HARD
SENTENCES

crime fiction inspired by Alcatraz

edited by
David James Keaton & Joe Clifford

BROKEN RIVER BOOKS
PORTLAND, OR

Table of Contents

Advance Praise for HARD SENTENCES:

"Each story has merit, whether reflecting the solemn hopelessness of the concrete tomb or capturing the essence of the inmate experience. An exquisitely moody, searing assemblage of tales, each distinctively contributing to the atmosphere and desperation of The Rock."

— Kirkus Reviews

"*Hard Sentences* is a gut-punch of an anthology centered on the most legendary prison of them all, written in blood and bile by a vicious gang of the hardest-boiled crime writers working today. All it's missing is Clint Eastwood and Don Siegel. So what are you waiting for, your next parole hearing?"

— Scott Phillips, award-winning author of *The Ice Harvest*

"I dare you to open this book to any story, read the first few lines, and not be instantly captivated. Trust me, I tried, then finally surrendered. Every single story is tight, bold, unique, and wild. Every single voice is authentic and compelling. Every writer has the storyteller's gift and an ear for the human heart. Do yourself a favor. Read these stories. And go directly to jail."

— David Corbett, award-winning author of *The Mercy of the Night*

"These 19 looks at the old penitentiary at Alcatraz are not just a great idea for an anthology, but a selection that is alternately stirring, poetic, magical, and bare-knuckled gritty. I liked it a lot."

— Ron Hansen, award-winning author of *The Assassination of Jesse James by the Coward Robert Ford and The Kid*

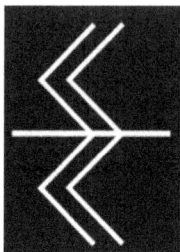

A Broken River Books original

Broken River Books
10660 SW Murdock St
#PF02
Tigard, OR 97224

Cover art copyright © 2017 by Joel Vollmer
Cover design by Matthew Revert
www.matthewrevert.com

Photo credits © National Park Service, Mark Rapacz, Nikki Guerlain, and Amy Lueck

Interior illustrations © Tony McMillen and David James Keaton

Interior design by J David Osborne

Les Edgerton's "Dream Flyer" was originally published in *Monday's Meal* (University of North Texas Press, 1997)

Mark Rapacz's "Bodhisattva Badass" was originally published in *Les Toiletttes D'Alcatraz* (Blastgun, 2017)

ISBN: 978-1-940885-37-7

Printed in the USA.

"The degree of civilization in a society can be judged by entering its prisons."

— Fyodor Dostoyevsky, *The House of the Dead*

"Break the rules and you go to prison. Break the prison rules and you go to Alcatraz."

— Anonymous

Introduction:

Slam Dunk at the Mesoamerican Ballgame (or No Escape from Planet Alcatraz)

by David James Keaton

When I first sat down to write the introduction for this book, I was a little sad I couldn't just write a story instead, but everybody was saying it was bad form to contribute fiction to an anthology you're editing. But then I realized what a perfect position I was in. All I had to do was write a story anyway and just claim it was true, the opposite of all great fiction. Or at least something all good intros should be, right? And by lying my ass off like this, I'd have snuck a short story right through the back door, snuck it *into* prison, you could say, something only a madman would attempt. It's not like anyone reads these introductions anyway. And if you really start thinking about it, this set-up is the perfect cover story if what I'm about to tell you actually did go down. Which it did, while researching the fiction I was going to pass off as true, everything happened exactly as I described. Confused yet? Just wait!

It was about three years ago when I first moved to California that I heard about the Red Bull-sponsored "King of the Rock" basketball tournament being played at Alcatraz, and the idea for this book hit me like a bolt of

1

lightning, or at least a regulation-inflated basketball to the face. Seriously, they were playing one-on-one games right there in the prison yard, where so many inmates had done the same (although 2/3rds of the Alcatraz prison population was white, so the games probably took a little longer). And when I heard about this tournament, first, I wished I'd been born with any sort of basketball skills whatsoever, but sadly, the only thing I was worse at was football, and after that, everything else. My only moment of triumph after three years of football in a very football town was turning off the boombox in the locker room right before the song "In the Air Tonight" hit the big drum moment, resulting in a bunch of seniors plowing me into a fence at the next practice and holding my feet off the ground until an assistant coach reluctantly made them set me free. The closest thing I probably got to experiencing prison, come to think of it.

But in basketball, I didn't even have that kind of highlight reel. Except that one time I wrestled away a jump ball, displaying my amazing ability to travel. The coach even came up with a name for it, "Keatons on the Feetons," a story I told my nephew, who then told his Jr. High football team, who all started using it during practice, meaning that phrase was adopted three states away and translates as just "fucking up" in general. Better than a goddamn trophy.

Now, since I'd never taken the infamous Alcatraz Island tour, I figured this was a good way to kill two birds with one stone. I had zero chance of actually playing in the basketball tournament, and not just because I wasn't one of the Top 64 players in the world and therefore not allowed to set foot on the court, but because I was terrible, remember? But I did get that jump ball once. And it seemed to me that you could wrestle a ball away from anyone if you wanted it enough. Also, I knew I'd have to do this soon because there was a rumor that the tournament was ending, actually moving to Chichen Itza next year, to be played at an actual Mayan temple? Or maybe I was conflating two dreams I'd had. Either way, I knew it was now or never. So I slammed a couple Red Bulls to get my mind right and bought my tickets. One for the tour and one for the tournament. 575 bucks, though the Red Bulls were free.

Side note: I knew a guy who drove one of those stumpy little Red Bull trucks, and he had cases of the stuff he gave away. I took some, too, though I'd never been a huge fan of the swill, probably because I drank too much to stay awake during all-nighters at a radio gig about ten years back, and one night, halfway through Bob Dylan's "Hurricane" (a prison song, of course, but more importantly, a song all DJs used to run to the toilet, a move facilitated by the drink itself), I'd finally pinpointed that unique taste. Blueberry-infused aluminum assholes. Seems like a weird sponsor for a prison basketball tournament, or any tournament, for that matter, but I'm no scientist. And, hell, prisoners make wine in their toilets.

Anyway, I arrived on Alcatraz way early, taking the first ferry out at 8:30 a.m., more than time enough for the tour before the first tournament bracket got started at 3:00 that afternoon. And as soon as I saw the graffiti and the crumbling buildings and heard the echo of the boat horn as we bumped the dock, I was mesmerized.

Alcatraz Island. I couldn't believe. Stepping onto it from a boat also amplified the exoticness of the place. See, I watch a lot of movies, and I knew they'd filmed a bunch of them right around my feet. What movies? Well, *The Rock,* of course. *Escape from Alcatraz,* of course. *Birdman of Alcatraz,* of course. But other lesser-known hits like *The Enforcer, Murder in the First, X-Men 3, Point Blank, White Men Can't Swim* . . .

Speaking of, one of the things I learned on the tour was that those famous stats about no one escaping from this prison were not quite accurate. By all accounts, several inmates made it to the water. So I guess it all depends on your definition of "escape." Like if you're eventually shit out of a shark in a fine, gray mist and finish your end-zone dance by dusting the coral at the bottom of the San Francisco Bay, that's almost as noble of a finale as your loved ones scattering your ashes off a fishing boat, isn't it? At the very least, it should definitely qualify as *getting out.* I feel like this should be included in the brochure.

It was about halfway through the tour when I saw the heads.

Replicas of the heads anyway. Vicki, the tour guide, explained that in the early morning of June 12, 1962, Clarence Anglin, John Anglin, and Frank Morris tucked homemade dummy heads into their beds and slipped through a ventilation shaft, surfed down a pipe, climbed two barbed-wire fences, inflated a raft made of prison-issue raincoats, and then paddled off to freedom. Or death (semantics). Nine days later, the search party found remnants of their shredded, makeshift raft, but even if they were capsized by the powerful Bay currents within minutes, they would have been free for plenty long enough for it to count.

And it was these freaky heads that ensured their escape, the tour guide reminded us. And he let us each take a turn filing through the cell to get a good, long look. They'd been meticulously constructed just as carefully as Morris and the Anglin brothers had masterminded their own doppelgängers, crafted from a papier-mâché-like mixture of toilet paper and soap, marbles for eyes, specifically milky blue-and-white onionskin "aggies" that Frank Morris always carried for good luck, a couple haphazard white Chiclets for teeth (they were Southern boys with Southern smiles), and then topped off with swatches of human hair swiped from the prison barbershop floor. The hair on the replicas looked more than a little bit like Burt Reynolds' worst wig, from his *Smokey and the Bandit II* era, not like his perfect square head in *The Longest Yard,* filmed at Georgia State Prison, by the way, which is no Alcatraz and has a shit-ton of successful escapes. All in all, it looked a lot more like Clint Eastwood playing Frank Morris than the actual Frank Morris, so that's a bit of symmetry anyway.

Back on the tour, I think I gave Vicki the slip right around his tales of "Times Square," and right then I knew I was going to steal one of those fake heads. I wasn't sure why I was doing this, to be honest, except that I was new meat on the West Coast, and maybe I really wanted to make some sort of impact, and maybe they'd still know my name around the island, now decades after it closed? *If* I got caught. But all I knew for sure was that it seemed important to set one of those heads free, if only for a second . . .

Who am I kidding? I was on Alcatraz Island, goddamnit! Where they filmed *Point Blank*! Maybe I just wanted to immortalize something as insane as that movie on camera. And the King of the Rock tournament was being carried on at least three Mexican cable stations. I'm not stupid enough to try and get arrested, but I'm not above a little high-profile vandalism. And if there's somewhere that should welcome a little vandalism, it's Alcatraz, right? You know all those movie crews fuck up all sorts of stuff while they're filming, right? And there's renovations on Alcatraz prison every year. At this point, there's probably no original brick left. Certainly no original heads.

Briefly, I considered making my own head at home and coming back to swap it out. Just smuggle one to freedom, then take a picture of it on the ski lift at Lake Tahoe, or a reasonably expensive seat at a Sharks game, on tour like a "Flat Stanley." That would have made more sense. A little planning and nothing would have turned out like it did. But, ironically, it was the idiocy of my plan that saved me in the end.

I lingered around the hallways with the tour still within earshot, hanging out in section near the church that was undergoing restoration. Through one of the windows, I saw the camera crews and basketball tournament organizers streaming off the ferry, and I knew I had about an hour to figure out the caper.

And somewhere around this time is when I remembered the only other tour I ever took in my life, at the Denver museum of Natural History, and their freaky exhibit with the Aztecs playing basketball with someone's godforsaken head. Okay, not an actual head. They don't use real heads in museum exhibits, unless you're an unlucky Chinese political prisoner on tour with Bodies: The Exhibition, forever dancing with another freeze-dried cadaver with a matching bullet pucker over your ear, or that poor bastard who had his skull incorporated into the "Arab Courier Attacked by Lions" exhibit at Carnegie Museum in Pittsburgh. But despite Denver's display curators having the good sense not to use actual corpses, it was still pretty terrifying.

The diorama depicted the famously brutal Mesoamerican ballgames of the Mayan civilization, similar to the less-brutal

Incan version, but not as high-scoring as the horrific Aztec version, where prisoners and high priests indulged in the ancient precursor to modern-day basketball. And, yes, they did this with heads.

I'd always thought this was a myth, but according to Bobby, the tour guide, they first started filling their crude animal-skull balls with goat bladders to give them a better bounce, which made the games faster, so that the losers got executed a lot quicker. Then they switched to using human bladders, Bobby explained, plucked from the bodies of the sacrificed players themselves. Now *that's* two birds with one stone. Our bladders were smaller and had more "spring" in them, she said. Then she pointed us to the restrooms.

I also learned it was the Spanish during their conquests who'd first witnessed the severed heads of prisoners being used in place of balls. They didn't have the rebound of those early balls, but you can't really go back to goat-bladders after a prisoner's face smiles at you all the way through the hoop.

It just had to be prisoners, right? Endlessly exploited throughout history, I imagined the guards playing the game with them, the red-faced bulls doing clumsy alley-oops. It was the perfect prison metaphor I needed for this book, prisoners turned to sport, much like Alcatraz turned into a tourist attraction, how simply being internalized in movies, books, and song was little consolation.

I stuffed a head under my shirt and ran outside. I think it was Frank's.

Then I hit the Yard so we could watch the game together.

It was some time during the slam-dunk contest and watching all those cameras swooping around to follow the action that I realized what I was going to do. I no longer wanted to merely smuggle a head to the mainland and freedom or whatever. Instead, I was convinced I needed to run Frank out onto the basketball court and chuck him through the hoop. Don't ask why. My dad, who coached girls much better than me at the sport, warned us once that a slam-dunk was worse than pointless. "It's a story in the middle of a song," he said. "And no one wants to hear that shit."

But a slam-dunk contest at Alcatraz made more sense to me than the current game of one-on-one. A regular game is burdened by gravity, you see. And there's an understandable obsession with flying among prisoners. Or wings. In fact, the only thing a prisoner is more likely to grow from his back besides wings is the handle of a sharpened toothbrush. But you couldn't blame sky-gazing birdmen from haunting crumbling jailhouse halls when Spaniard Juan Manuel de Ayala, the first European to explore San Francisco Bay, christened it *La Isla de los Alcatraces* in 1775, a name Vicki explained meant "Island of the Pelican." Not really, but his translation was close enough. But it is true that the Rock was a lot more rock-like back then though, with very little greenery, and seabirds preferred this rubble to civilization.

There's something about islands. Combine an island with a prison, and you've got a recipe for mythmaking, like the stories you'll find in here.

Except maybe for Rikers Island. That shit feels man-made, especially after they hooked the artificial satellite "Vernon" to it. A prison barge is slumped, uninspired, listless, like something bobbing around in a *Waterworld* outake. Because, at the risk of being the asshole who always says, "It's not 'Frankenstein'; it's Frankenstein's *monster*," Alcatraz was always the name of the island first and the prison second, so, in this case, the monster does share the name of its father. And that makes all the difference.

I plotted my dunk strategically, remembering from my Denver tour that the original Mayan hoops were stone, and that they were sideways, like someone had grabbed the rim for their dunk and cranked it like a doorknob on the way down. So this shit should be way easier, I decided. I considered trying to hang on the rim, too, but it seemed like an impossible goal. Running out and slamming that head through the hoop would be victory enough.

So that's exactly what I do. True story.

I take three big steps, traveling all the way, then sailing up, up, and *slam*. Crazily, once the head clears the hoop, the damn thing keeps going, bouncing once on the foul line, then out of the Yard, then up and over the nearest wall, seeking every story it can find, through a window and into the prison library and past the photo-op where Whitey Bulger famously got his tourist photo taken while he was on the lam, and from there the head pinballs through the shower heads, down to the dock, and under the pier, where it rolls over a millipede, leaving a glow-in-the-dark comet streak across a dusty cheek like war paint, then it ricochets off the lighthouse and launches past the graffiti on the water tower, still bright as blood from the occupation, sailing high over the guard tower where Joseph Bowers was shot climbing the fence, for a quick lap across the entire Bay, where the head dodges the shadows of the almost 2,000 jumpers since 1937, their bodies flash-burned into memory as they pirouette off that blood-red bridge with the unlikely but complicit name of "Golden Gate," until the head's orbit brings it back around, skipping the Pacific Ocean like a stone, off the noses of sharks and gannets and all the way back through a broken window to swirl around the shower drain that routinely collected Al Capone's blood while he wept, past the rope where they dangled the key before the riot, before it finds its home back under the sheets of Cell 138, where it takes the place of Frank Morris himself, becoming him easily as he vanishes from the planet forever...

The pull of that tractor beam is no joke. The San Francisco Bay might be the closest thing our country has to its own Bermuda Triangle, with more than a hundred shipwrecks due to its strange weather, a perfect storm of strong currents, thick fog, and a reef as sharp as any jaws. I know how an island is *supposed* to work, anchored to the Earth and not bobbing there in the water like bait, but somehow this island seems simultaneously more and less stable than that, as if the mirror image of Alcatraz really does extend beneath the waves, as if the symmetry of this rock spins imperceptibly on its own, exuding its own gravity, letting no one free, no matter how hard they swim.

Planet Alcatraz.

After those historic Mayan ballgames, there's still some debate as to whether they sacrificed the winning team or the losing team. Which seems like something that should have been agreed upon before the game started or you'd end up with some serious *Blue Chips* point-shaving incidents, but maybe these games were where point-shaving originated, at exactly the same time as basketball itself. Not surprisingly, they also invented the first three-step rule, to avoid Keatons on the Feetons, I presume, but their games only went to eight points. Coincidentally, that's exactly the same number of points I scored all through high school. Exclusively foul shots. Hey, at least they weren't underhand, like that kid in the wheelchair in *Hoosiers*.

Intro: No Escape from Planet Alcatraz

Speaking of underhanded! Okay, time to come clean. I can't dunk for shit either. You already knew that. So the head didn't go on adventures. Here's the truth of it, since this is an introduction and not a story. Instead, Frank's head came down on the rim, and those white Chiclets went everywhere, like Frank had been curb-stomped. And the rim tore through the head much easier than it would have torn through an actual skull. Or so I'm told. But what I'd done, and what saved me from being charged with whatever crime that might be, was I'd inadvertently proven this fake head was more like a real head after all, hidden in a plain sight in a National Park where over 5,000 tourists passed by it every damn day. Not a real *human* head, of course, because that would be fucking bonkers. But for whatever reason, the dummy head from Frank Morris' old cell contained the skull of a coyote, presumably for heft? Or maybe shape? Or the smile? Who knows. But this revelation, combined with the cherry-preserves filling that topped off the ridiculous prop, was realistic enough to get referee whistles blowing and children screaming, and me and my almost Vaudevillian handful of pie I was still holding got us both hustled off the court and into the old guard tower for questioning. The actual guard tower! I was swooning.

Later that night, I heard that 36-year-old L.A. native Tarron "The Beast" Williams won the tournament and the $20,000, and he was crowned the final "King of the Rock." I can't remember who got the thousand bucks for winning the slam-dunk contest, but I still feel like I'd earned an honorable mention, at least. TVs recorded none of my feat, however, or if they did, the tapes were destroyed, as the National Park Service was already working hard to deflect rumors of prison tours decorated with bona fide human remains.

This is why tours rarely give details of the grisly Mesoamerican ballgames, and only whisper of the blasphemous Mayan slam-dunk. Because prison is weird enough already, you know? And if *White Men Can't Jump* taught me anything, it's that if you're palming a human head like a basketball, especially if you're down by one and going up for the final shot, or doing something as stupid as telling a story in the middle of a movie, or if you clear your throat and flap your arms like wings when your only task is to write the introduction for a collection of stories that can more than speak for themselves, only a fool would try to show off.

Break
by Glenn Gray

The first self-inflicted fracture was the middle phalanx of the right fifth digit, but that was just a test. It didn't matter because it would have nothing to do with the job. Bone snapped easily with just a slight jerk, as if cracking a knuckle. It fractured swiftly and effortlessly, and surprisingly without much pain. I'm no stranger to fractures. A good part of my childhood was spent in hospitals and doctor's offices, showing up with bones broken due to forces that seemed no greater than a strong gust of wind. It started early on, as a toddler, and continued into my teens until things got sorted out. I always figured my bone issues were probably why I chose to become a doctor in the first place, thinking it would give me some kind of control, of which I had none.

I was born with a mild form of osteogenesis imperfecta, better known as "brittle bone disease." Genetics gave me bad collagen. Fractures were a regular occurrence, a routine part of my life, and the whole thing didn't make for a particularly active or happy childhood. I probably shouldn't complain too much because children born with more severe forms of the disease typically don't make it past their first month.

And it turns out, my brittle bones, in conjunction with my medical knowledge, became quite useful when I arrived at Alcatraz in July 1941. I laugh sometimes thinking my bones were also why I was there in the first place, angry at the cards I was dealt, huge chip on my shoulder. But that's a horse of another color. This story, the one about the prison, won't be found in any history books or newspapers, but it should be because I'm the only person ever to escape from Alcatraz and survive.

Well, sort of.

The first key was that the warden took a quick liking to me. My appearance was unintimidating, and I could be charming and affable when I wanted. My face had the classic physical features typical for the disease: triangular in shape, with a broad forehead and mild mandibular prognathism, or subtle underbite. The whites of my eyes had a blue tinge. But if you passed me in the street, you would think I was sort of funny looking and probably carry on, forgetting you ever saw me. I was average height, only achievable with mild forms of the disease. And due to prior fractures, my arms and legs had slight angulation deformities. My chest also had a barrel shape. And I possessed mild thoracic kyphoscoliosis. All in all, a perfect storm of impediments.

The next key was that I was a well-respected physician prior to incarceration, albeit with anger issues. I made sure I was a model prisoner and behaved myself, easy with the "yes, sirs" and the nods and smiles. As a result, the warden singled me out. Not infrequently, he called me to his house in order to attend to minor medical issues for him and his family. He seemed to value my opinion much more than the prison docs that were usually just out of training, and besides, they never lasted that long, running back to the safety and tranquility of civilian life at the first hint of danger.

The real reason he requested me was his daughter, Mindy. Most people weren't even aware that she existed. It was obvious to me the warden was ashamed of her and kept her hidden. I was often called to treat her physical ailments, like pressure sores, contractures, and bouts of mild pneumonia. She was twenty-one when I first met her. Her body was ravaged by childhood polio, but I thought she was beautiful. The first time we met, I saw nothing but warmth, and I knew right away she felt the same for me. It was as if we connected through our deformities, our ugliness a response to the world at large.

Apart from the bones, I had other medical issues, things I didn't divulge. I didn't want any unnecessary attention or questions, but I also had celiac disease, an intestinal malabsorption disorder. As a result, my intestines had problems absorbing calcium and vitamin D, a double whammy with the brittle bones, but a blessing and a curse, as I later discovered.

The celiac disease was also the main contributor to my pale, anemic coloring, a lack of vitamin D and B12, adding to my odd appearance. Because of my unusually white skin, I was referred to as Casper the Doc by fellow inmates, like the cartoon, or sometimes "Doctor Ghost." Eventually it was shortened to just "Casper."

I had been taking phosphates, vitamin D, and calcium supplements for years, in order to help prevent fractures. That and exercise, mostly walking and swimming. But when I arrived at Alcatraz, I stopped taking my supplements and cut out any dietary sources of calcium. I avoided the sun at all costs, wrapping myself up like a mummy anytime I was in the yard, as sunlight was necessary for vitamin D activation, something I was now denying my body. Everyone thought I was weird and quirky, which was perfect. Inmates kept their distance, and the warden thought I was a harmless loner, but my overall goal was two-fold:

I would lose weight and allow my bones to revert back to their tragic, weakened state.

As I sat in my cell and fractured my pinky finger, it dawned on me that I was ready. Sitting there on my cot, I shifted the fracture fragments back and forth, embracing the sense of freedom this new motion signified. It was the dead of night, and I glanced at the dinky sink, metal toilet, the 5x9 foot space and thought, *20 more years? No way.*

Pinching the middle phalanx on the opposite hand, I gave it a swift twisting jerk. There was a soft snap and another new motion.

The fragments, now as free as their brothers, glided right past one another.

I noted a subtle skin bruise at the fracture site, much less than normal, likely because the bone had diminished vascularity, and as a result, less oozing.

I stood. Shuffled to the bars. Grabbed cold metal with both hands, evaluated the width once again. Turning sideways, I passed my arm through to the shoulder and assessed the depth of my barrel chest. Turning forward, I pushed my face into the space between the bars, the metal squeezing my skull and my head stuck at the junction of the frontal and parietal bones, just above the squamous portion of the temporal bone. This was good.

The horizontal cross bars were a definite nuisance and

created a dilemma in that the overall height of the space was cut in thirds, so I would have to squat and straddle my body to get out. Options were going out headfirst, frontway, or legs first and backwards. I needed to think about that. I put a leg through sideways until the bars met my pelvis. Anteriorly, the pubic symphysis would be an issue, so I made a mental note of the width of my pelvic girdle.

After full analysis, I sat back on the cot and set about doing some serious fracturing. Each night for two weeks, I fractured the same bones over and over, not allowing them to fully heal, but instead building a soft bridge of callus. I fractured the fourth through eleventh ribs on each side laterally, resulting in a vertical line from the armpit down. Each snap was easy, a short push with a fingertip, sometimes three pushes, each time a little harder than the last, right before the pop. These fractures allowed the front half of my rib cage to ride over the back half, like some kind of bony piston, and narrow my thoracic cage significantly.

The pubic bones required multiple fractures, two spots on each side, given the osseous configuration of a pelvis was akin to a pretzel, so it wouldn't normally deform. I had to fracture both the superior and inferior pubic rami. This allowed the front half of the pelvic girdle to ride past the posterior portion, and, like the chest, narrow the front to back dimension. These fractures were hard to achieve given their location. I couldn't just push like with a rib. I found the best way was to squeeze between the bars and force myself in until the cracking started. First on the left, then right.

The hardest part was the skull.

I only did it once, to make sure it worked. I had to be careful the fracture line didn't extend into the squamous temporal bone and lacerate the middle meningeal artery.

The result would be catastrophic, ending up with an epidural hematoma, death almost instantaneous, my head probably outside the bars straddling my neck when I was found cold and stiff in the morning, like I'd hung myself between the metal. Embarrassing. I was not suicidal.

The skull fractures needed to be horizontal and high, so the inferior bony plates would push in under the superior plates, narrowing the key part of the calvarium. I did this by sitting alongside the cot, pushing the mattress away to expose the metallic edge, then imagining a line along the calvarium. I whacked my head sideways into the metal edge over and over, like some kind of desperate mental patient, of which I was neither.

It was the hardest fracture of all to achieve. The calvarium, even diseased, is thick and built to protect from exactly what I was doing to it. Eventually, it fractured. While banging the opposite side, in my excitement, I knocked myself unconscious on the fourth and final blow. I woke up on the cold floor in a daze, staring at the ceiling, just in time to crawl back in bed before the guard's perimeter walk.

The final key was Mindy. I said we connected immediately, but it was much more than that. We were in love. I knew from the moment I was called over to treat a decubitus ulcer on her lower back. Her left leg was paralyzed, the right partially, and she had poor sensation from the waist down, so she often developed pressure sores. One of her arms was severely spastic, causing her elbow and wrist to curl forward. Surprisingly, she was able to walk well with a cane, despite the bulky metal brace on her left leg.

When I arrived that first time, she was on her stomach, and I evaluated her gaping wound. Bad decubiti are typically hard to look at, even for a doctor. The smell, the pus, the dead skin and exposed flesh and bone. When she rolled over though, our eyes met and it was glorious. All I saw were her eyes, wide, stunning, symmetrical orbits, full of wonder. She gazed at me and our line of vision was awkwardly locked in place, like a tightly tethered clothesline, until the warden, who was standing nearby, cleared his throat. He knew right away what had happened, and I believe he was pleased. He must have been, because I was asked back, again and again, and my love for Mindy deepened each time. We shared only one furtive kiss when we were alone for nine glorious minutes, but that was enough.

Over time, I whispered to her my plan to escape, and we spoke about spending the rest of our lives together once I was free. But first, I needed her to do one thing. I needed her to hide a raft and life vest at a particular spot along the shore on a particular night. She resisted at first, but ultimately agreed. After many evenings in the library, I became an expert on every current, tide, and weather pattern around San Francisco, and, specifically, around the Rock.

When I finally chose a week, a day, and a time, I was so excited that I almost risked cracking my knuckles.

On the night of the escape, I fluffed and arranged blankets and clothes in my cot to appear as if I were sleeping. Approaching the bars, I put my right leg through and shifted until my pelvis stuck. My original plan had been to go through legs and pelvis first, then chest, and head last, but I changed my mind at the last minute. I would put my arms through first, as if diving, then my head, then squiggle the rest of the way through. If I was able to pass my skull through first without a problem, then I figured I would be fine, and the rest of my body would follow me to freedom.

Withdrawing my leg, I got on my knees. I extended my straightened arms out, palms together, and slid them through the bars. I twisted sideways, but turned my head so that I was face out. My skull met the bars and stopped. Snug. I was able to bend my arms back and grab the bars from the outside, to get some traction, and I shifted my legs so that my feet were on the floor, bent as if at a track meet, ready in the starting blocks. Firming myself up, I waited a moment and took a deep breath. Closing my eyes as I exhaled, I pushed and pulled and heard the crackle of cranial plates, and a lightning bolt of pain flashed through my head as my brain squished inward. I actually felt my brain pulse, as if it was drawing breath, as I grew dizzy.

A dribble of saliva leaked from the corner of my mouth right before I passed out.

I woke a few minutes later, I think. I couldn't tell how long I'd been out, hanging there between the bars, but I hadn't been discovered, arms and head dangling, my worst fear. I regained my bearings and returned to work. I shimmied sideways so my sternum pressed against one bar, and my back, at the mid thoracic level, was at the other. I braced myself with arms and feet and pushed until I couldn't move anymore, and with a victory grunt lurched forward. With loud snaps, crackles, and pops, the anterior and posterior halves of my rib cage shifted over each other and choked the air from my lungs, compressed my heart so I was lightheaded again, and short of breath, pulse stuttering like a backfiring car. I thought of Mindy, and my heart grew tight as a fist.

And as I passed through the bars and the rib cage retracted outward, the air pulled in with a great whoosh and rivers of blood re-expanded my heart and it sped back up like a jackhammer. I hung there, slumped sideways up to my mid abdomen now. It took me a half hour to regulate my body and convince my organs to stop their revolt and regroup.

Eventually they agreed. We were all in this together.

Needing to work fast now, I wriggled and heaved my pelvis in between the bars, locking it in place. This awkward position made it harder, didn't allow for a good thrust from my legs, still thrumming in their starting blocks. I would have to rely more on arm strength, of which there never was much. And there was new pain growing in my chest with each movement.

I managed to get a hand around a bar, the other palm flat on the floor, and I inhaled and exhaled deeply as I yanked forward. The bones didn't move. I rested a moment and tried again. This time I tried harder, and I heard a crunch, but it wasn't enough. I waited a moment and sensed something, and when I looked around, I saw the prisoner next door glaring at me in horror. I brought a broken finger to my lips, imploring him to remain quiet, but something like a boat motor erupted from my mouth. He just shook his head at the ghost suspended between the bars, maybe a sight not unfamiliar to a prisoner after all.

I drew in a deep breath and knew that this time it had to work, as men were waking up, and I was running out of time. I thought of Mindy again, and pulled with all my might. I couldn't get a short quick pull, which was preferable, only a long, drawn-out motion, but I didn't care, as I heard the crackling and grinding of bone on bone and the shift and thud which compressed my bladder and sigmoid colon.

23

Urine and stool leaked from my body as I passed through with a triumphant but protracted groan.

I fell to the ground with my ankles draping the cross bar, the not-subtle smell of bodily fluids seeping upward into my nostrils, mercifully jarring me awake like smelling salts. My breath hitched and coughed, each inspiration accompanied by shooting pains into my chest. But I couldn't let that bother me. I clambered to my feet, clutching the bars for assistance and stood tall a moment, gathering myself, the prisoner on the other side of my cell now wide-eyed and agape.

I started to stumble towards a sliver of sunlight and the promise of vitamin D activation in the distance, pelvic bones clicking with each step, wobbling like a damaged puppet, limping, grasping the bars for support. Up ahead, a guard walked away from me, headed toward the cell that housed the staff restrooms at the end of C-Block. I quickly turned and started the other way, toward one of the two doors that would release me forever.

And when I got to the barred door, I repeated the whole procedure again.

It was so much easier squeezing through the bars this time, given I was warmed up and the bones were freshly broken. But what really helped, besides that flicker of sun, was the adrenaline pouring through my body, endorphins streaming and dampening the pain.

Eventually, I made it outside, dazed, and I slowly staggered down towards the water, my body drinking in the sun I saw the tumble of boulders up ahead. Then I saw the yellow raft and an orange flash of the life vest Mindy had hid amongst the rocks and brush. I dragged the raft toward the water and could smell the sea salt as the cold air slapped my face. I found myself at a small ledge, a drop-off of about three feet to the sand and water below.

"Stop!"

I turned and saw two guards a couple hundred yards away, moving towards me, guns drawn.

I reacted instinctively, thinking I could kick out in the raft far enough into the fog before they got to the water.

And I jumped.

Under normal circumstances, this would not have been a problem for anyone. But in my condition, it always was. I knew I'd made a mistake as soon as my feet left the ground, and the split second before I hit felt like an eternity.

My knees shattered simultaneously, followed by both tibia and fibula, fracturing and collapsing in multiple sites so my kneecaps plunged all the way down to my feet. Both femurs drove upward, first breaking above the knees as they hit the ground and subsequently pushed up through the acetabuli, with the femoral heads jutting up above the iliac crests, resulting in two grotesque soft tissue bulges at the low back, to join the new distortions pulsing at my hips.

My torso folded forward, like a closing book, multiple ribs splintering as my chest hit the ground, finishing up in a heap at the water's edge. Sand rode a wave into my mouth as my face hit, and overwhelming pain seared my body. I struggled to move an arm, my hand reaching out to the icy water lapping at my fingertips.

When one of the guards ran up, he stopped abruptly, befuddled at the contorted, gnarled pile of flesh and bone sprawled on the sand. He was unsure of what he was seeing, and it took him a moment to process. And after a tense pause, he uttered, "Mother of God." I caught a glimpse of the raft riding off without me, and I closed my eyes to block out the sun. Traitors all.

Technically, I escaped from Alcatraz on an emergency medical ferry, and I was hospitalized for a year. My body was hideous to most, deformed beyond belief and beyond repair. And given the situation, what I had tried to do, my case was never given top priority. I remain bedbound and contorted, catheterized and diapered.

But because of Mindy's petitioning, along with her father's begrudging fondness for me, my contorted form being possibly the closest approximation he'd ever had to a son, I was granted something like a pardon, essentially paroled early, which didn't matter because I wasn't going anywhere fast in my condition.

Mindy and I lived together as she took care of me, and we both hid from the sun out of habit, but, truthfully, we no longer had any need for it. This went on for twelve years, until recently, when she passed due to complications of pneumonia. The warden had died several years before after a major stroke, but for as many days as we had, Mindy and I loved each other dearly.

It is only now, with both of them gone, and the island and its crumbling, cold fortress relegated to a tourist hotspot, that I am able to reveal this story as per an agreement with the warden. Not a legal agreement, but more of a gentleman's agreement, which I respected. I have no doubt I should be in the history books, somewhere next to Houdini, who died from suffering far fewer injuries than my own, and even the warden believed this to be true. But it's okay. My body doesn't hold a grudge. I can't even hold a pencil for very long. And all the anger drained from my skeleton and muscles long ago. I lived and loved, and I was happy for a while. But more importantly, I escaped.

The Children and the Gardener

by Amber Sparks

To us, he was The Gardener. No name, just The Gardener. Funny that, because of course there were many gardeners, many groundskeepers. Some were lovely to us, some odd, some gruff or taciturn, and one would flash a smile all black with missing teeth. But The Gardener was the only one who'd earned the capital "T" capital "G."

We all knew when someone had escaped, had flown or climbed the fence or fallen off the cliffs. The red would flash. We could see it from our bedroom windows, flooding the rooms with lurid light. They always brought them back, sometimes dead, sometimes not. You could never quite see the bodies, but we all pretended we had. We liked to lord it over the mainland kids, the things we'd seen. We imagined ourselves quite jaded.

We kept watch over the waters in the direction of Angel Island—we hoped for a makeshift raft of escapees—or bodies, bloated and purpled, bumping over the waves. Our fathers would shake their heads, and frown, and forbid us the binoculars we had asked so many times for. Our mothers called us morbid. They whispered to our fathers in the hush of prison dark, was this any kind of life for children? Was it fit? Would we grow odd, crooked, end up right back here to end our days less free than we began them? Our fathers, who herded hard and leathered men through days and nights, would laugh. They would kiss our mothers, and they would sometimes bring death to men and sit to dinner hours later. The commute, they said, could not be beat.

We were just like other children in most respects. But we did not fear monsters under our beds, or shadows along our walls. The monsters, we knew, lived just down the hall, locked up tight.

We didn't know what The Gardener had done, though we made many guesses. The eldest of us was sure he was an old gangster, long past his heyday of running rum and whiskey and gin. The youngest of us was sure he was a bank robber, the kind the cops were always chasing on TV, blam blam blam. A long string of successes behind him, locked safe after locked safe sprung, and then—caught up like a fish in the law's wide net. We were never quite sure whether we cheered for the police or the robbers, and mostly, we cheered for both. It seemed the surest bet.

He was stooped, white-haired, with the skin of someone standing long years in the sun. He seemed frail and strong at the same time, steady of purpose and with large, deft hands. His eyes were no color you could tell, no matter how long you looked—they were blue and green and brown and sometimes black, and often they were the sky and clouds and all the fierce waves of the bay. There was a fierceness to him, too, that sometimes made us uneasy when alone with him too long—though it seemed an alien notion, nothing to do with us. He was as inscrutable as snow.

The most of us thought that he might be a murderer,

strangling ladies with those big, long hands. But the oldest of us scorned the most of us utterly, rolled their knowing eyes past the cliffs to the Bay. Our fathers, they said, would never let him near us had he done such things. The most of us shivered with fear and delight, anyway. We wanted to be uneasy in our friendship with The Gardener, unsure of where we stood.

He built us things with those hands. Teepees and forts and stout little slingshots, playhouses and cribs for dolls. Hobbyhorses and rocking horses and bright painted signs for our clubhouses. Like the others, he was always planting cuttings on the hillside terraces on the west side slopes, and he carefully tended the rose garden. He told us the soil came from Angel Island, and from the Presidio, long before any of us had ever been born, even he. Back, he said, before there ever was a prison here to die in.

Sometimes, he told us stories. Strange short stories, unlike any we'd heard in nurseries or books. They seemed wrong somehow, and sad, and they seemed to be missing an ending or a moral. We didn't know what to make of them. Just think, he would say, there were days when the world was brand new. Can you imagine, he would say. This is how he always started his stories.

Just imagine, he said to us once. Death no sure thing, not back then. Humans might live for hundreds of years, only to be called up to the Other World in seconds. Sometimes the dead were allowed to choose: remain with the living, haunt the earth, or sleep forever. Sometimes the living forgot the dead; sometimes they remembered every nail and skin flake, each expression and birthmark.

Would you become a ghost, he asked, if you could? And we ran home to our parents, hid from the sun, safer near the

31

cruelest locked-up criminals than this odd man. He seemed to belong to some Other World himself.

Our fathers supposed him quite harmless, though he made our mothers nervous. Despite the harshness, the brutality of the island, our fathers believed in rehabilitation. If a man could find good, honest occupation, they felt. If he could only turn the dirt with a rake or a hoe or his own two hands. They never said what, exactly, would follow, but it seemed the good earth offered up second chances.

We did not believe in second chances, nor rehabilitation. Children rarely do. A monster is a monster, we knew, and the only good monster was a dead monster. Some of us lived in the prison proper, and some of us lived in the outbuildings near. The prison dwellers outranked the outlanders, and all of us outranked the mainlanders. They were white and soft, pale as milk and just as weak. We were tough, and ruthless, and we were smarter than most other children. This we knew, this we told ourselves.

Can you imagine, he told us, when the world was new, there was a great city by the sea. He was tending the roses, long fingers deft around thorns, and we trailed behind. Hanging wary on his words.

In this city by the sea, he said, there was a man, a very wealthy man. And the man loved children, so much that he never wanted to be without them, even in the Other World. And so when the man's time came to choose, he chose death, and he chose the children's company, too. He paid the people of the city a great deal of money for their children. Then he gathered all the children to him, and when it was time to go, he pulled them close and took them all with him into death. And so the city lost its children forever.

What happened, the boldest of us asked. Did the parents cry? Did they miss their children?

No one cried, he said, not then nor ever again, for the city's punishment was swift and severe. A wave, taller than ten thousand buildings, rose from the sea and swept that wicked city away. And all the wicked parents with it.

Were the children happy in Death, asked the shyest among us, small-voiced. But the man did not answer. His fingers were bleeding, his brow wet with work, and we nodded sagely at one another.

Our parents came with sorrow eyes, tried to comfort us with candy and kind words. Our parents told us The Gardener had gone, though they did not tell us how or why. Our parents let us listen to our radio programs until late in the night, and tried with clumsy hands, with soft stubby fingers, to build us a tree house. It collapsed under the weight of the first small storm.

We thought the roses looked bent, and sad. We thought the terrace gardens wilted and wept. But we thought of the man, his body rolling, smashing fast down the cliff face, sinking in the waters of the bay. We thought we had done the right thing, and we said so to one another. We nodded. We told each other a story: imagine, we said, an island by the sea. Imagine the children of that island grown strong, grown wise. Money meant nothing to the children. Roses meant nothing to the children. Promises, gifts, kind words—these meant nothing to the children at all. The only thing the children cared for was the children, and the wild beauty of the island, and both were safe for now, for well and good.

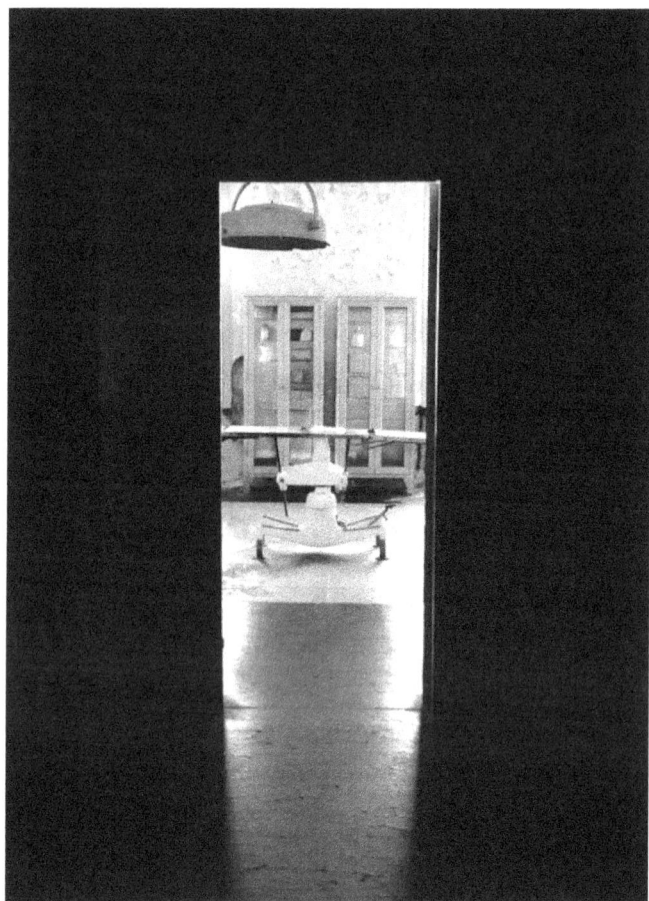

Being Whitey
by Nick Mamatas

It wasn't Alyssa's worst trip, and as acid goes it wasn't even especially weird, but there was something about this one that made her spinal fluid bubble and squeak. She could smell the sea, and a distant trace of fried foods. She felt different; her limbs were longer, stronger. Alyssa was a man now, her belly full of chuckles. He was having a good time, posing with his girlfriend in comically exaggerated prison garb, a lightweight ball and chain. An Alcatraz Island tour staffer took their photo. He liked wearing the prison-issue cap; no giant bald dome in a picture for a change.

A thought emerged: *Fuck these fucking fuckers, the fucks.* It came out in her own voice, with her own accent, and the trip was over. Government-issue LSD was always rough; it felt something like the beginning hours of strep throat.

"Well?" the agent asked Alyssa.

"He's in San Francisco. Actually visiting Alcatraz. Like a tourist," Alyssa said, half-choked, desperate for water.

"Bulger's always been audacious," the agent said.

Alyssa didn't know what that meant. "Well . . ." Alyssa said, a whole question embedded in the word.

"Well what?"

"Uhm . . . aren't you going to make some phone calls? He's at a famous landmark. Right now!"

"Is he?" the agent said. "Was someone walking by with today's *San Francisco Chronicle* while you were . . ." he paused, struggling with something internal, ". . . experiencing his experiences? Where was the sun in the sky? It's early morning out West."

Alyssa didn't know exactly—and didn't know how she knew—but no, it hadn't been the morning. The sensation was . . . lunch. He'd had a full belly. "Yeah," she said, her lips twisted.

"It's good intel anyway," the agent said as soothingly as he could while still retaining a sense of the imperious and disinterested. "A public place, a national park. Potential photographic evidence as well. Easy enough to make calls."

Alyssa shifted in her reclining chair. "If there is a picture, could I see . . ."

"No," the agent said.

Of course not, Alyssa thought, then and also later when she was back at her usual haunt in Harvard Square. *It would ruin the experiment.* So many things could potentially ruin the experiment: Alyssa had money now, but couldn't use it to get a real room in a real apartment. She wanted to kick her other habits, but couldn't—what if her visions weren't thanks to just the LSD, but to the whole pharmacopoeia she ingested over the course of the average week? At the same time, she couldn't just up her intake and tell the feds to screw off. The one time she tried, a half-dozen black sedans swarmed down Mass Ave. and busted her dealer right in front of her, mid-exchange. He went away and, unlike most low-level street workers, stayed away, which was good since he would surely be gunning for her as a stoolie when he got out of jail.

Purple cough syrup. Alyssa still called herself a "street kid" at twenty-six. Irish whiskey, which may as well be running out the taps in the apartments Alyssa couch-surfed through. The booze helped her deal with the headaches. An assortment of pills, most probably nothing, but pretty-looking, and fresh from a friendly fat guy's pocket in exchange for a handjob. She wasn't a prostitute, or what the kids at Harvard called ever-so-politely a "sex worker." Alyssa just had a handful of friends she liked to spend time with and have sex with, and they sometimes gave her money because she needed it. Sure, she had an address, in Swampscott, but her mother was a total bitch, so she was hardly ever there, okay? Then before she knew it, it was Monday again—every day was a weekend to Alyssa, so Monday always snuck up on her—and she was fetched by her handlers and deposited back in the gray building, a paper cup of water in one hand and a smaller paper cup with an LSD tab in the other.

A big black swirl, that's how the trips always started. It unnerved Alyssa. She told herself a story, that the inky cloud of nothingness was the beforetime—before Whitey Bulger had volunteered to be part of the MKUltra experiments while in prison in Atlanta. For all the good it did him; a smiling guard told him, "Enjoy sunny California, with all the fruits and nuts," and it was a long ride across the country to the Rock.

Today, he was looking in the face of a real-life "frickin' Red Indian." His voice reverberated in her synapses. It wasn't something he said, but experienced. Clarence Carnes, the Chocktaw Kid was a kid, literally. At least a decade younger than Whitey, and he was in for life after fighting it out with the bulls, and then the *frickin' Marines* at age nineteen, during the '46 Blastout. Whitey was still a kid himself in his early 30s; his mother was alive and he couldn't bring himself to even think the real f-word. Carnes had a voice that soothed, even when he was talking about the blood running from the holes in the men at his feet back in '47. Everyone in Whitey's life was always bellowing. When Carnes talked about the happy hunting grounds awaiting all the good people, and even most of the bad people, Whitey felt his head buzzing, his spine tingling. Carnes's story always ended the same way: ". . . most of the bad people, mind you, except murderers. They—" never we, no matter which murderers had gathered 'round to listen—" are kept out, just close enough to hear the music and the laughter, to smell the bison roasting, to catch a glimpse of the tan breasts and thighs of the women . . ."

Sounded better than Hell, which is where Whitey knew he was headed one day, and forever.

Hell was murky. When Alyssa came back from the trip, the FBI agent tried hard not to look disappointed.

"Are you a reader, Ms. MacLeod?" he asked.

"I wouldn't go so far as to say I am, officer," she said, getting a little fancy.

"I'm not an officer."

"Whatever, mister," Alyssa said.

"That's right out of any number of biographies of Whitey Bulger is my point," the agent said. "Are you even seeing into his past, or just telling me some story you read about?"

She shrugged. "I'm not the book type. Wasn't last week's experiment a good one? A real 'hit'?"

The agent didn't even try to hold back his sneer. "An Irish girl from Southie never read a book about Whitey Bulger, or

taking care never to even step across the streets on the sawtooth border between towns.

Now Alyssa understood, or thought she did. Same genes, same drugs, but maybe now she would be able to tell present from past, to really experience what Whitey was experiencing, instead of just remembering what he'd already experienced. The FBI agent came for her on Monday and brought her to the gray building, let her check her phone to guarantee that the money had been deposited into her checking account before relieving her of it for the afternoon, and gave her the usual dose.

Alcatraz was Hell; Alyssa knew it like it was a fact stitched into her skin. The Chocktaw Kid's friendship and protection wasn't always enough. Even that rambunctious kid had to sleep some time. Alyssa *felt* what happened, and it felt huge, and like burning, like Hell, swelling up from behind him. Worse even than the headaches. Whitey Bulger promised himself that he'd never go back to prison, except to piss on those frickin' SOBs. When he got out, he'd be staying out. There was that other Hell, too, the one much further away, under the waves, under the Earth, that lasted forever. Whitey Bulger would happily march down into the lake of fire to stay out of the hell he'd already experienced.

Whatever it took, it took. Kill some of the boys he came up with—sure, if he had to. Turn fink and feed the FBI a few tidbits in exchange for protection—why not, the feds were easy to play. Kill a woman—why the *fuck* not? Whitey's mother was five years dead when Stephen Flemmi's "stepdaughter" Deborah Hussey got herself arrested for turning tricks, maybe got all chatty with the local police while cooling her heels in the holding cell. He could think the f-word now. He could think anything he needed to do. There's hell, and then there's Hell.

Whitey had a sense he was being watched. Always somebody, always something. Had the feds put something in his brain during those experiments? A capsule-sized electret microphone? Yeah, he knew something about electronics, too. The throbbing. *Hussey*—yeah, that was an apropos surname. Whitey had a good vocabulary. Better than Alyssa's. He was smarter than the average Southie mick. He knew things. He knew he was being watched.

Whitey looked in the mirror. He could still see the girl, even though his eyes were watering from the pain in the back of his head, in his reflection. She was a big-haired blonde with that familiar Irish dumpling face, and though he was seeing her through a glass darkly, he knew it had to be Hussey. She was the one causing the headaches, working with the feds. And through the mirror, and the years, Alyssa stared back at Whitey, and knew this would be her last trip. Hell was forever, and she was in it. Time had very little meaning here. But when it came to that one moment in time that meant something, the moment when Whitey clamped his hands around the girl's throat and start choking while the man she called "Daddy" waited in the vestibule, Alyssa was watching through Whitey's eyes, strangling with his fingers, on a strange throat that wasn't her own, but that as she gagged and sputtered and the world went black, felt like it was.

Dream Flyer
by Les Edgerton

They *never* bust cock fights—least-ways I never heard of it before—hell, half the spectators is always cops—but here I was, in the Orleans Parish Jail, and here I would sit my butt another ten days. Twenty down, ten to go.

I'm not one to bellyache, but it just ain't fair, this roust. I was just there, as a sort of observer of the human melodramaticus, not betting or nothing, and the judge sentenced me anyway. I might have five lousy bucks or so down, but that was it. A hundred, tops. Hell, some'a these players light their Cubans with a C-note!

I even brought up my college education to the honorable barrister, but that didn't cut no grass.

"Your Honorable," I says, "I've got nearly a full semester in right here at our own Delgado J.C. and woulda finished up pret near the top'a my class, only there was that ruckus at the Saints game you mighta read about, landed me in the clink right before mid-terms and that washed my higher edification right down the spigot. And," I tacked on, "I only made a general comment about our famous quarterback, which I might add, half the town agrees with, having

45

witnessed with their own eyeballs ol' Junebug Taylor out and about the party trail powdering his nose over to Pat O'Brien's before the home games, and besides, I never laid a glove on the other guy as he had me down and tromping about on my rib crate before I knew which end was sideways, and it wasn't my fault twenty or thirty other hotheads jumped in and began mixing it up and got the security guys involved in stuff that wasn't none'a their bidness."

I figured he would see the logic of my calculations when I further explained that since I was bum-rapped on that litigious, I figured the state owed me one, but not this bailiff, no, he just raps his little hammer down and says, "Mr. Thierry, you've been before me four times in the last year and a half and you still don't get it, do you? Thirty days! Call the next case. By the way," he leaned over as they were leading me away, "it's water down the *drain*, you nitwit, and my report says you were flunking both your classes. How do you flunk fizz-ed, lessen you're in an iron lung?"

So much for the value of an education these days.

All of that was awhile ago—a year, actually—but I thought I'd stick that in so's you could see how it all started out and how I'm really an innocent dupe in all this.

Some other things happened in there you might not know. How, ten days before I was to be let go, they put me out on a work detail, picking up go-cups the tourists had rudely thrown on the ground, and I kind of walked away, being distracted by a little honey with some serious hot pants who I know wanted me to come over and pat her on the po-po, which I did, and which resulted in a charge of escape and some other trivialities, which got me sent over to the Farm in Angola. Escape! Can you believe it? I walked ten steps away from the doofus hack and just to give my respect to those hot buns that were screamin' at me to pat 'em, and that's *escape*?

Granted, when I walked off the work detail at the Farm and they chased me through some pretty miserable swamps and other such hardships, that might be construed as escape and I don't deny it, but that's when they sent me here, to The Rock, and the judge says, "Let's see you escape *that*, you moron!"

Well, I'm here now and they also give me a life sentence on account of I accidentally killed one of the guys chasing me in the Achafalaya with his coon dog and it was truly a random accident as I only meant to render him unconscious with the sleeper hold I applied, only he musta had a weak constitution as he went into a deeper nap than I'd intended and so all that's why I'm here, looking out at the City by the Bay, which is S.F., home of the Seals and Joe DiMaggio and all the interestin' stuff.

And then, they had the effrippery to put me into the same cell as "The Dream Flyer." That's what I called him, right from the gitgo—you probly read about him in the *San Francisco Weekly Shopper* and thought some reporter give him that name—but it was my oneself that named him, not no booze-hound with a typewriter. What happened, one of the other inmates—that fruitcake bird guy, I think—let it out that's what I called him, and that's how he got his brand.

His real name, which you might not know, seeing as how the papers always call him "The Dream Flyer" now, was Karol Block, with a K, not a C, but which don't matter nohow, since nobody remembers his real handle no more. It was in all the papers, even up in Oregon. Nobody likes a child molester, but everybody sure likes to read about the skunks!

I probly know more about him than his own mother, who didn't much cotton to him to t'begin with, bein's she usta crank him over the head with the cast iron fryer when she was in a mood, and so never did any serious confiding in, like he done with me. Being cellmates makes you closer than Siamese kittens, and what I don't know about Karol wouldn't take three minutes to foretell.

"I'm gonna beat the rap," he says, first day I checked in, and I only half-heard him as every man Jack in here's gonna beat that same rap. "I raped her, sure, but I didn't kill her. I wasn't even close to her, being knocked out and disambulatory. She kilt herself. Got up and run into a tree branch, knocked her inta the river which she proceeded t'swalla half of, not having taken the caution of closing her trap like anyone with any sense woulda done." He was talking about the twelve-year-old moppet he was in jail for rendering extinct in a particularly gross way. He had glommed onto a new trial for that, but didn't want to talk about the three guards he'd killed in other prisons which got him sent here to Alcatraz. I think he figured he beat his original rap, they'd just dismiss the others—that "fruit of the poisoned chinaberry tree" legal thing.

I shook my head in sympathy cause that's what you do in jail; you agree like you was up for reelection, 'specially if you're in the same cell as a mad-dog killer. Not agreeing with folks makes 'em mad, and jail is no place to get someone PO'd at you, 'specially a ice-cube cold rape-killer like Karol. You can't just walk away and climb on a bus, happen they take exception to something you say. So I agreed with him most of the time, even at his craziest, which was generally all the time, maybe arguing on some minor point just to show him I was no pushover, but a tough tomato, same as him."

"I got a plan," he says, meaning to beat the rap, and proceeds to let me in on the scam. It seems laying in the joint gets him to remembering about when he was a juvie, and he comes up with this idea that when he was around seven or eight, he could fly. The story he gives me is that he could get out of his body, like a pearl-diver shucks his wet suit, and float around and buzz around into other rooms to check if his parents was playing bedsheet tag or what-not, and one thing leads to another, and pretty soon he figures out how to fly while still in his body, by holding his breath and suspending his molecules and some other tricks and deceits of the trade. First time, he finds this out accidental, when he was nine, when he jumps off a little hill and finds he can stay in the air longer than other kids of his same general weight and height classification, and then, by a lot of practice, he gets to where he can take off from a flat spot and go clear up into the clouds, dodging aircraft and flocks of robins and spy satellites and other such artifices. Kind of a nine-year-old Superman, 'cept he didn't have any X-ray vision or incredible strength or work on the *Daily Planet*. He could just fly. Then, he claims he got older and interested in girls and lost the art.

"You shoulda kept flyin," I says, cracking wise. "Girls is what got you into this fix," but when he doesn't laugh, I drop the subject like a match burned down to the tender part of the fingers.

I asked for another cellmate, but they said no, they was overcrowded. I can help fix that problem, I come back; give me my walking papers, but Whitey the hack only walked away giggling and shaking his head like he thought I wasn't serious.

After giving me this look that makes my blood turn to

Kool-Aid, Karol tells me that he remembers all this flying business from his own youth again, under the stress of the predicament he's in, and not only that, he's been practicing every night and has regained his powers. He's been in Alcatraz almost six months before, working out with the aeronautics, so he's up to the point of loop-de-loops and fer-de-lances, or so he says. Since I only been here a few weeks, I can't attest to all this, but I think one night I seen him raise up off the floor a couple two-three inches, but then it might have just been a mirage-a-twa, since I seen my ex-wife Dixie at the same time, sitting over in the corner on the stool, doin her regular occupation which was boffing her nails, and besides, I had drunk a half-pint of apple-jack I got for two packs of Camel regulars, maybe half an hour before I dozed off which mighta had something to do with what I was visualizing.

Dying don't bother him none, Karol says, but getting exterminated for something he didn't do, gets his dander up. He done the rape, sure, but it warn't his fault she run into a tree and kilt herself, is his take on the deal.

Weird, huh? I had to stay in there, across the bunk from him and pretend the puzzle that was his brain had all the pieces.

His genius plan was to wait till his big day when they take him to Sparky, when they take him to the little room where they pop the needle into you, and just up and fly away from 'em. Then, he'll come back and let 'em give him his shot. This will prove his innocence, he says, and also show them that dying don't mean a hoot in a pile of owlshit in the mote of his eye, and he can die joyous.

Well, there is some squirrely folks in the joint, and I've met a couple of 'em, but the Dream Flyer, he's an originaldiginal if I ever come across one, with both cheeks fulla walnuts and pecans.

Least he was. Yesterday was the day they was supposed to extinguish him, and they even let me go to a conference room and listen on the radio for when it happened. All the stations had remotes there since it was such a big deal and one of those days the governor hadn't accepted a bribe— slow news day is what they call it—and I guess the turnkey thought me'n Dream Cookie was bosom sidekicks since we celled together awhile, and so I got to go up and listen with Whitey and the other moron hacks. Beats laying around in your six-by-ten, winking at your trouser worm and teaching it to sit up and do tricks.

Well, believe it or not, he never made it to the death room. Course you know that unless you've been living out in Sacramento or the Okefenokee, cause that's all that's been on the tube since.

He fell and broke his neck, is what it said in the *Examiner*, but they wasn't real clear about what went on, only that he fell three tiers and squashed himself like a Halloween pumpkin off the overpass. Neck-breaking was the official cause of death, but the way it sounded, there wasn't a bone left in one piece. He went from Dream Flyer to Dream Whip. Instant parole.

Now, all this has got me to putting my thinking cap on. The way I figure it, there's just the skootch of a chance that the Dream Flyer was onto something. I even disremember something way back when I was in short pants myself, a time when I used to get out of my body and float around the trailer. Thing is, I can't tell if I really remember something like that, or if talking to the Dream Flyer makes me *think*

I remember it. But the more I cogitate on it, the more I'm sure I done it.

Starting tonight, I'm gonna start practicing. See if maybe I can get out of my body a little bit, for a few minutes or so, maybe fly over to the chow hall and get hold of one of those steaks the cooks save back for themselves, cop a piece of that sweet tater pie they claimed they was out of. Maybe go over to the Anglin brothers' cell and see if they really do have that escape plan they keep yapping about in the showers. If it works, then I guess it's possible to fly. I remember everything the Dream Flyer told me about suspending the molecules and such, and if it's possible, I can do it as well as he could. *Better*, I hope.

If it's possible, think of the feasibilivities! I mean, there's not a joint built that could ever hold me! I'd like to see that judge's face, next time I stand up there for some cockamamie crap like gambling. I'd fly up to the ceiling and wave at him right before I shoot out the window.

"Hey, judge," I'll yell. "I believe I'll do those thirty days over on the Redneck Riviera over to Panama City."

That's the kind of *statement* I'll be making.

Let's see, Karol said you suspend your molecules And do something with your breath . . . Damn! This is gonna be easy! See how the justice system likes it, playing on an even field.

Color my ass *gone.*

The Sympathizers
by Rory Costello

April 1865

Schadenfreude had long been life's prime delight for Samuel
Parks. Yet the sensation had never been so sweet. Glad
tidings! The Illinois ape, Lincoln, had been shot. About
damned time, Parks mused.

Parks knocked the dottle out of his corncob pipe
and packed a fresh bowl. He fired it up and drew slowly,
contentedly. The whiskey tasted mellower, too, as he began
to compose his editorial for the next day's edition of his
newspaper, the *Buena Vista Partisan*. Parks had earned his
nickname—"Prattle"—because he never would shut up. He
wasn't about to start now.

"A Man Reaps What He Sows!" the banner headline
proclaimed. Six paragraphs of inflammatory sour grapes
followed.

Much of Buena Vista was pro-Confederate—indeed,
there were secessionist hotbeds up and down California.
But the pro-Union populace was outraged. Armed with

crowbars, axes, and torches, a band of townsmen razed the
Partisan's offices.

Word of the incident spread quickly, and the U.S. Army
responded. A force of 20 soldiers on horseback rode into
Buena Vista to restore order. They found Parks gazing at
the still-smoldering ruin of his building. The Army captain
moved his horse forward a few paces.

"Samuel Parks?"

"Who wants to know? State your business, blue belly."

"We have orders to detain him."

The captain handed Parks a sheet. Parks snatched it with
a contemptuous snort and read:

Headquarters Department of Pacific
San Francisco, April 17, 1865

General Orders No. 27

*It has come to the knowledge of the Major General
commanding that there have been found within the Department
persons so utterly infamous as to exult over the assassination of
the President. Such persons become virtually accessories after
the fact, and will at once be arrested by any officer or Provost
Marshal or member of the police having knowledge of the case.
Any paper so offending, or expressing any sympathy in any way
whatever with the act, will be at once seized and suppressed.*

By command of Major General McDowell.

R.C. Drum
Assistant Adjutant General

Parks looked up. "McDowell?" he said, cackling in perverse glee. "Irvin McDowell? The bungler of Bull Run? The one who wore that damned ridiculous helmet? But yep, I'm Parks—and I'm exulting, all right. 'Utterly infamous' is a good one, too. This Drum fella can turn a phrase. Anyway, you're just a *leetle* bit late to seize and suppress. The mob already did a good job of that. So what else you gonna do?"

The captain's response was simply to turn and tell his men, "Clap him in irons."

A burly sergeant and three other wolfish soldiers dismounted. As Parks railed in fury, they shackled him and marched him out of Buena Vista.

Similar arrests took place elsewhere around the state. In Manteca, Anthony Markham had capered down Main Street, giving his version of a rebel yell and discharging two pistols into the air. The county sheriff handed him over to the Provost Marshal's staff, and Markham made a grueling hike of 75 miles west to San Francisco.

In Punta Arenas, up the Pacific coast, Richard Potter was apprehended for echoing John Wilkes Booth's cry of "*Sic semper tyrannis!*" He was thrown into the cargo hold of a schooner and left in the dark for the duration of the sail down to the Bay.

Down south, in Monterey, John McManus was just as intemperate. With the better part of a fifth in him, he announced, "The horrid-looking wretch had it coming years ago! The world is well rid of its greatest scoundrel." In one way, McManus had it easier than Markham and Potter; he was placed aboard a steamer, and his trip was quicker. He was put to work shoveling coal ash, a taste of what was to come.

One curious case took place in Humboldt County when

dressmaker Nellie Masters, not wishing to befoul the streets of Eureka, fashioned a diaper for her white mare from an American flag. Though she was arrested, as a member of the fairer sex, she was released with merely a reprimand.

All in all, more than 40 Confederate sympathizers from California—excluding women and children—were taken into custody for rejoicing over Lincoln's murder. Their destination: Alcatraz.

Captain William Kindell was a man of indeterminate age with scanty blond hair and no beard, unusual for the time. This kept his hallmark creepy smile visible at all times. Kindell had assumed command of Fort Alcatraz the previous year, and the ongoing development of the fort continued, with Army engineers in charge.

Lieutenant Richard Barnes oversaw the work crews, which had included a number of Union soldiers who'd been sent to the guardhouse for various reasons, along with assorted other military prisoners. Kindell had summoned Barnes to his office to inform him of the incoming batch.

"What's the most prisoners you've had working for you before?" asked Kindell.

"My guess is 10 to 20," Barnes replied.

"We don't guess in our line of work, Lieutenant. Guessing gets men killed. We *estimate*."

"Indeed, Captain. Military science," said Barnes, thinking, *You pompous twit.*

"At any rate, Barnes, you're about to get some reinforcements. Quite an influx—at least 40, I'm informed. Their boat is due in shortly. Do come with me to greet them."

Kindell and Barnes walked to the wharf, near where

one of the new projects, a bombproof barracks, was being constructed. The launch full of prisoners arrived and was moored. The guards escorted the sympathizers to an assembly point near one of the batteries, where Kindell addressed them.

"Allow me to quote a great man," said the captain, amused with himself as ever. "'Work, work, work, is the main thing.' Do you know who said that?"

Parks had the answer. Naturally, he couldn't hold his tongue. "The idiot!"

The odd grin remained on Kindell's face. "Who?"

"The baboon!"

Kindell remained tolerant. "I know who you mean, but would you kindly refer to him by name?"

"Not for all the gold in California," Parks growled. "I don't speak it or write it. I wouldn't even piss it in the snow."

"A man of principle," said Kindell. "I admire that. Your principle shall be tested here, Mister . . . ?" He let the question hang.

"Parks."

"Thank you, sir. Does anyone else care to venture the answer?"

None of the other prisoners responded.

The captain let the silence linger a few beats longer, before continuing. "Mr. Parks is correct. It was the man who brought us all here together—Abraham Lincoln himself." Kindell took relish in the looks of disgust that swept across the faces of the sympathizers. "Mr. Lincoln spoke often on the subject of work. And work you shall."

"And if we shan't?" asked Parks.

"Splendid question," said the captain. "I'm very glad you brought it up. The alternative is warm accommodation—

the warmest we have to offer. It can be quite chilly here, but you'd never know it."

"If I may, I'd like to regale you with another tale featuring our esteemed late commander-in-chief. Two years or so ago, the president visited one of our Navy's steamships. He was shown a sweatbox and told that it was used for insubordinate sailors. He insisted on trying it for himself but could endure no more than three minutes. Forthwith, he ordered the Secretary of the Navy to ban the practice aboard all vessels flying the American flag."

"But this is not the Navy . . . it is the Army. And with respect to Mr. Lincoln, some infractions require more stringent measures, as do some places. This is one of them."

"For the privilege of expressing your opinion, you will engage in the tasks we set you until such time as you see fit to recognize the opinion that matters most—the law in these United States. As Abraham Lincoln said, 'Labor is the true standard of value.' By that token, gentlemen, you *will* prove your worth."

Lieutenant Barnes and his men assigned the sympathizers to three different crews. McManus and Potter were sand packers: their job was to fill 60-pound jute bags with sand to reinforce the bulwark at the Presidio. Markham was a rock breaker. Parks was a digger: his crew was excavating the foundation for the bombproof barracks. They were all hobbled with ball and chain. If that wasn't humiliating enough, they had to work in view of visitors to the island, including children, who pointed and snickered.

At Kindell's direction, the soldiers paired Parks with the most annoying partner available, a lewd-minded Union prisoner named Norton who was even more voluble. In particular, the former farmboy from Indiana held forth endlessly on the subject of "public women" and his carryings-on with them.

"Christ, Norton, I'm no Puritan, but you're making me sick," Parks grumbled. "Will you shut your hole? I think syphilis must be eating your brain."

"Not me, buddy," said the Hoosier. "I always wore a skin. They weren't so easy to get, though, so I hadda keep washing 'em out."

"Enough! I don't want to hear another *God . . . damned . . . word.*" Parks longed for a smoke. Remarkably, his pipe hadn't been confiscated, and he even had a little baccy left in the pouch. But he didn't have a single match. It was maddening.

"Okay, okay. No more whores. But I got other good camp stories for ya. Wanna hear about the grayback races? Them cooties can scoot!"

After just two hours on Day One, Parks had had it. He picked up his 24-pound ball and dropped it on Norton's foot. Yet despite two cracked metatarsals, the farmer didn't cry out. Instead, he grabbed his own chain, swung the ball like a knight with a flail, and nailed Parks across the shin.

A guard spotted the action and ran over, asking, "What the hell's going on?"

Norton calmly lied. "He asked me to do it, Corporal. He said he didn't wanna do no work for no Union sonsabitches."

"Well, *why'd you* do it, you stupid bastard? What's in it for you?"

Norton shrugged. "It's not like I got nothin' to lose. Y'already got me for ten years. Can't make my sentence no longer or harder."

Parks was writhing in pain, yet he perked up a bit. Prison hospital would be boring, but it beat this ditch digging—and it would get him away from Norton.

Kindell's unsettling grin was still fixed as Parks—in a temporary splint—was dragged before him by two beefy PFCs known as "The Ox Team."

"Mr. Parks. It would appear that you don't place the same premium on the value of labor that Mr. Lincoln did, and, in the here and now, that I do, as well. We take a rather dim view of malingering in the U.S. Army."

Parks tried to spit but couldn't gather it from his dry mouth. His voice was a hoarse mutter. "You takin' me to the doctors?"

"In due course. We don't want to see you lose that leg. Just to let you know, though—even with it in a cast, you should be able to dig quite effectively. You should have asked Private Norton to swing for an arm. But meanwhile, we have a little discipline to mete out here."

"Sweat box?" asked The Ox Team.

Kindell nodded.

"Take him."

It wasn't even fit to be a coffin—two-feet deep, two-feet wide, and just a little over five-feet high. It had just a one-inch hole bored in the top to admit air. One of the Oxen crammed Parks inside. Although he stood just five-feet-six, Parks still had to bend. The lid was drawn down tightly, muffling the shouts and imprecations.

The temperature on Alcatraz seldom got above 75 degrees, but The Rock was sometimes at its balmiest in April and May. Soon Parks was drenched. He felt nauseated and headachy. Dizziness followed. He yelled and pounded on the lid but to no avail.

When the lid was pulled off the box, after not even half an hour, The Ox Team found Parks unconscious and covered in vomit. They each dumped a bucket of cold seawater on him. This revived Parks, and got his core temperature down.

The damage, however, had already been done. Heatstroke caused Parks' speech to be slurred; he suffered hallucinations. He was allowed to remain in the small frame building behind the guardhouse that held all the additional prisoners. But a few days later, he had a series of seizures, and The Ox Team carried Samuel Parks away, never to be seen again.

The remaining sympathizers wondered vaguely what became of Parks. Some speculated he'd been buried in one of the pockets of rock that had been blasted out to make way for gardens—a few of them were freshly filled with imported soil. Others figured he'd just been dumped at sea. Another theory held that he'd been put away in an Army asylum. The Oxen were no longer around to talk either; the word was they'd been mustered out.

Lieutenant Barnes looked vainly for written orders, and next of kin for Parks. When he asked Kindell about it, all he got was a sigh and a platitude.

"This War Department bureaucracy, Barnes. The reams of paperwork. It's—how shall I put it . . ." The captain glanced up at a quizzical angle, searching for *le mot juste*. "*Augean?* You wouldn't want to get bogged down in that muck, Barnes. Be happy you're an engineer, not an administrator." The subject did not arise after that.

Meanwhile, the sympathizers just kept their heads down—digging, breaking rock, and packing sand. They stayed at it for several weeks, 8 to 12 hours a day. Finally, in mid-June, they were ferried across the Bay and brought to the U.S. District Court in San Francisco. There they stood trial for their use of disloyal language toward the government. It was all just a technicality and went swiftly. The judge found them guilty, and the men were compelled to take an oath of allegiance to the United States of America.

"Now repeat after me, gentlemen. 'I do solemnly swear . . .'"

Most of them were genuinely humbled by the whole experience—but three expressions were anything but solemn, ranging from a sour grimace (McManus), to a roll of the eyes (Potter), to a smirk (Markham). And as the men enacted the charade, they remained unrepentant. Sedition still infected their hearts and minds.

"'. . . that I will support, protect and defend the Constitution and Government of the United States . . .'"

The South shall rise again, Markham thought.

"'. . . against all enemies, whether domestic or foreign . . .'"

Federal government is the true enemy (Potter)

"'. . . and that I will bear true faith, allegiance and loyalty to the same . . .'"

Secesh to the bone (McManus)

"'. . . any ordinance, resolution or law of any State, convention or legislature to the contrary notwithstanding . . .'"

States' rights forever (Potter again)

"'. . . and further, that I do this with a full determination, pledge and purpose, without any mental reservation or evasion whatsoever . . .'"

Markham wasn't the only one crossing his fingers behind his back.

"'So help me God.'"

To the Devil, thought McManus as he parroted the final words easily—they were the same number of syllables.

As they walked out of the court building, free men once more, Markham stopped for a moment. "Say, I was just thinkin' again about that Parks character. Ya think if he hadn't lost his mind, he coulda gone through with this?"

Potter shook his head. "Never in hell. He'da sooner cut his throat with a rusty razor."

Even without the sympathizers, work continued at Fort Alcatraz. The foundation for the bombproof barracks was dug out, and the last remaining task was the cement. But before that final pour, Barnes looked over the lip of the trench and tossed in a small object he'd found in the room that had last held Parks. It was a corncob pipe, its stem cracked.

Construction of the building was abandoned in 1867, after only the ground floor had been completed. The Army assigned both Kindell and Barnes to new posts. In another of his aphorisms, President Lincoln once said, "Half finished work generally proves to be labor lost." But that wasn't true in this case. In 1874, a wooden barracks was added on top of the unfinished structure. And in 1905, it became Building 64, which housed newly arriving military officers and their families.

Many of The Rock's residential buildings have since been torn down, but Building 64 still stands today—it's the first structure one sees upon docking. And for more than a century and a half, there remains an oddity. People standing in a certain spot have sometimes reported an audible rapping—like a plug of dottle being cleared. And on those rare occasions when the winds off San Francisco Bay subside, those with an especially keen nose have even claimed to catch a faint whiff of smoke.

Clean Shot
by Jedidiah Ayres

Those last months with Gerty were awful, a funhouse inversion of our early days giggling and petting behind her mother's house in Kansas. We lived in heavy silence and terrible outbursts of anger and spite, grief all used up and left far behind. Her deterioration was easily tracked on her face, and I knew it would end badly, but I only watched, just did my rounds, accepting physical and verbal abuse as well as her hateful silences that went on for days in turn. It was exactly the way she'd described the last days of her parents' marriage. She wasn't sure when her mother was worse—drunk or dry—but she said it was some kind of relief when her father died and all that was left was the manic intensity of the beauty queen game.

I'd spoiled all that, and Gerty had loved me for it once. Those final months, though, she hurled it back at me with frightful violence that only got worse when, in moments of clarity, she heard her mother in her own voice. Then she would cry and say she'd rather die than become like that bitter old bat. I should have kept my mouth shut, but instead I agreed that would be the better outcome.

* * *

Joe Bowers had it hard. Unfit for free society, weird and unwanted, but doubly shunned in confinement where social circles were tightly shut and the warden's rule of silence kept the nervous fount of babble that he used to relieve some of that pressure stymied and capped. The guy was sick with nerves, friendless and strange. He was a born talker just like Gerty had been, so I listened to him. Better than I ever did to my wife.

With both of them it was a mental health thing, but with Bowers it never felt like a challenge to my authority or like some sort of test. It was easy. He said interesting things. Besides, Johnston's no-talking policy was primarily aimed at con-to-con fraternizing, so it was a gray area with us.

The first time he opens his mouth he says, "Belgium is cold, and so is Switzerland, but Russia? Fuckin' no thanks."

I'm supervising Bowers and Stoetzel on the janitorial shift one afternoon when I walk up to him.

"What did you say?"

His eyes widen in alarm as if to scold me that we weren't supposed to be conversing, before continuing under his breath and with his head turned away from me.

"It's cold and cruel and ugly, just like my Ma."

"Your mother?"

"Never knew her, and nobody talked about her, but everyone says Pop was handsome. And Spanish." He turned and smiled at me.

"What are you talking about?"

He stops his mopping and presents himself to me arms out like a fashion model. "I look like a Pollack or some kinda Beau-hunk blood. When I was in Russia, everybody looked like me."

When I don't respond, he continues.

"I don't look Latin is all. So I figure I gotta look like my Ma." He bends over his work again, "and she must've been an ugly bitch."

Paul returns then, and that's all the chatter we get until the next afternoon. When Stoetzel disappears around the bend again, I say, "So, you look like your mom?"

He nods. "The way I figure."

"Yeah, she must've been ugly."

That was the first time I saw him smile.

I was saving $10 a month since moving into the bachelors' dorm, but it wasn't going into any bank. I hardly ever left the island. Ate with everybody else, quit going to church, picked up my laundry on Sunday. Nights I'd have a beer and throw a few frames at the rec hall or take a walk down to the pier by myself. I wrote letters I'd never send, too. Mostly apologizing.

Feeling unusually social one day, I nod appreciatively when Montgomery picks up his split, the crack of the pins bouncing off of each other and the hard wood sounds like gun shots. I take a pull on my beer and stand to dry my hands over the vent before picking up my ten-pounder.

"You know Joe Bowers?"

Tom screws up his face for a second. "The, uh, postman?"

"Says he's been to Russia. Believe that?"

I cock my hip, and before I let the ball go, he says, "Guy's gonna ice somebody one of these days."

The seven pin jumps out and saves me from another gutter, and Tom nods to pretend it was a decent effort.

"Really?"

"Why do you think he's here? Stole what, twenty bucks? From the U.S. Mail so he's federally fucked, but not exactly the profile of our average con."

This time I knock down six more pins.

"You ever see him throw one of his fits? Got himself some time in solitary last time. Shouting gibberish, throwing rocks. Nobody knows what he was even worked up about. He's here 'cause he makes other cons, normal ones, nervous. Don't he make you nervous?"

I shrug.

"Most of these guys got friends or mothers or wives or something waiting for 'em, keeps 'em healthy, keeps 'em in line a little, but he's . . . squirrelly. Like a squirrel. Guys like that, they reach a breaking point. He does his stretch without blowing his top and killing somebody, I'll eat my hat." He bends over to tighten his laces as I take my seat again. "You ever seen Gowran's wife though? Imagine having to go home to that? Maybe Bowers is lucky after a—" Montgomery looks up at me, red-faced.

I waive my hand like it's nothing.

"Jesus, Ray, I'm sorry. Got a size-nine boot in my mouth over here."

He dumps to me the rest of the game, and he picks up our tab. I appreciate the effort, but the night's already a bust. I write another letter before bed.

Over the next couple months, I get stories from Bowers in small daily doses. Odd, bordering on fantastic, claims of being raised by circus folk, traveling the world, working as an interpreter in a half-dozen languages. I find most of it unbelievable and difficult to reconcile with the dumpy, middle-aged, former civil servant who'd violated the sanctity of the U.S. Mail, but once in a while, he lets slip a burst of nonsense that sounds like German or Portuguese curse words, and I do think he seems a little healthier for having our secret outlets of conversation.

I watch him in the mess hall, and it's like Montgomery says. No friends. Shunned or shy, I can't tell. The other cons stiffen a little when he gets near.

When he rotates off of janitorial, I hardly see him at all. Near the end of winter, I hear he's getting his head shrunk after a suicide attempt.

I found a suicide once when I was at Leavenworth. Strangled with his bed sheet, toes barely grazing the floor. Face was purple, tongue was swole. I didn't even check for a pulse, just blew my whistle and cut the poor bastard down.

Gerty didn't look anything like that when I found her on the floor. She still looked pretty. Empty, but pretty, lying on her back, even the spit foamed between her lips looked nice somehow. I'd stuck my fingers in her mouth, and then turned her over. I'd made a fist and pumped her guts, got her to cough up enough of the poison so her heart didn't stop. Doc Twitchell told me I'd saved her life, but I knew better.

Twitchell didn't think so much of Bowers's try. Said Joe'd had a real good shot at ending his life if he'd been sincere— he'd broken his eye glasses and slashed his throat with the shards—but all that he'd managed to do was give himself a tiny pink scar under his chin and get out of work for a few weeks.

Next time I see him up close, he looks like he finished the job. Sallow toned, listless, unkempt. When our rotations match up again, I can hardly get him say boo. Won't even look me in the eye.

This time I do the talking. Joe doesn't say anything, but he hovers near me as much as he can while he works. I tell him about Gerty.

I say she was a runner-up Miss Sunflower State once, only lost to Miss Wichita in '27 to go further. When we met, she was sixteen, and I was twenty-one, the son and grandson of farmers who didn't want to go into the family business. Gerty's old man was a consumptive who had moved the family to western Kansas before succumbing, and her mother never forgave him for taking them out of Chicago to the driest tit of the Volstead sow. Mom had been a dancer and planned to use Gerty's pageant purse to move them back east. While Gert's flapper frame may have won in a more cosmopolitan setting, Kansas standards of beauty still favored powerful legs and bust lines that took generations to cultivate.

When Gerty became pregnant, we got married. I got on at the prison, and we moved out of Ulysses to start our family. Her mother never forgave me, even though Gerty didn't lose her figure. As far as her mother was concerned, she was damaged goods. We lost little Dickie to a fever, and I won't talk about that, but around that time the Army sold Alcatraz to the Bureau of Prisons, and I put in to Warden Zerbst to recommend me for a transfer. San Francisco sounded exotic and as far away from bad memories as we could possibly get.

We made a run at it, too. Joined the Presbyterian Church, went out with friends Gerty made on the mainland where she got a job as a hostess. We may have had more children. I wanted to, and I'm pretty sure Gert did, too, but she was given to hard swings in her emotional state—happy as I'd ever seen her and full of hope, next thing I know, low and dull and hardly able to get out of bed. Occasionally violence visible in her eyes. I slept uneasy.

I asked Twitchell about her, and he said it sounded like fairly common female problems—that losing a child and moving across the country were bound to cause some disruption, and that she'd settle down soon. He said I should do my best to make sure she kept a regular schedule, and that I'd have my wife back any time.

But she didn't get better. The bad times got worse. Darker and more prolonged. She complained about everything and, like an unhelpful husband, I took every complaint as a personal attack instead of really listening to her.

Some of it was undoubtedly personal though. She said I'd stolen her away from the life she'd been destined for, she said her mother had been right about me and that she was just as much a prisoner as the men in the gray clothing that I was paid to watch.

We'd always enjoyed a drink, but she was doing it more all the time, and that was when I saw her mother beginning to emerge in my wife. I didn't say it, but she was thinking the same thing, and she knew that it had crossed my mind.

Some things I don't tell Bowers. Some things I keep to myself. Like I don't know if I believe in God. I have no idea what happens after death, but when I interrupted the attempt to end her life, I hadn't hesitated. If I had paused just a moment, I may not have kept her from dying, and she might now be at peace. Some say what she was doing was a mortal sin, and that she'd have passed on not in a state of grace, unfit for paradise, but that's not a certainty for me.

I didn't save myself any suffering, I'm certain of that.

I don't know if she still suffers, locked inside her body, unable or unwilling to speak, fulfilling bodily functions without will or purpose. I took her back to Kansas by train, and rather than sending my income to a sanitarium I pay Gert's mother to take care of her.

She finally got her baby back.

Bowers is on incinerator detail when I'm shifted to tower duty. I watch the men move in patterns like ants, single file along the grounds. The Bay feels like a fish bowl, and the wind is constant and bone cold. And Bowers is at low-ebb again, I can tell. He mutters and spits fitfully to himself, free to do so without fear of breaking the silence rule as long as he doesn't shout. It's a solitary duty.

He glances up at me, and I raise the fingers of my right hand off my rifle in salutation, but he doesn't recognize me or is not currently present in body, his mind wandering elsewhere, seeking who knows what? His ugly mother or handsome father? The traveling circus folk among whom he claims he was raised? A girl, like the Florentine flower retailer he claims he flirted with badly and pined for dedicatedly during a year in Italy, or the Lubbock prostitute he'd first transacted with as a teenaged boy?

Maybe he was spinning new stories from history imagined or lived. Freedom must have been on his mind, exposed as he was to the open air, his view of the world clear, obstructed only by a chicken-wire fence, but hopelessly separated by a seventy-foot drop onto sharp rocks and cold waters with impossible currents.

Johnston says that flight was pre-occupying his thoughts. He tells me this while we are alone in his office and he is shaking my hand. I don't contradict him, but the Warden insists that I prevented Bowers' escape, and that's where I disagree.

That day, as I watch the men move through their routines and Bowers burning the trash, I think of Gerty and her mother again, both of them trapped in that house with each other, their lives reduced to routines dictated by clocks, mechanical and biological, one mute and the other alone, and I wish I'd just let her go. I wish I'd let her die young and pretty and sad. I wish I'd turned my head and let her escape.

Just before he bolts for the fence, Bowers looks up at me and waves. Before I can return the gesture, he's hauling his dumpy frame up the wire barrier, his final obstacle. The warden will ask me to tell him again how many shots I fired. I'll tell him "three," and he'll nod.

The first, fired as a warning, draws the attention of the other guards, who draw their weapons and shout at the convicts on the yard to drop to the ground. The second I place near his head, but he doesn't slow down.

I sense Tom Montgomery preparing his own shot, and I shout at him to stop. It's my shot to take. Bowers hoists himself over the top of the fence, and climbing down the other side makes him face me.

No one who witnesses the incident will report this later, but I see the pleading in his eyes. When he pauses on the downside of his climb, it's believed that he didn't know which path to choose, which jump into nearly certain death, but I know that he holds still so I can get a clean shot.

And by God I do.

The Ballad of Easton Tucker, The Last Man Out (or Eat Shit and Die)

by Michael Paul Gonzalez

"Fuck the Anglin brothers, and fuck Frank Morris, too. Fuck Allen West, for that matter. Fuck this prison. Fuck this island. Fuck this country!"

Easton Tucker's words echoed off the wall in sharp buzzing notes, the fear of discovery long-abandoned. He inhaled, a sharp rasp as his leg slid deeper between the wall and a water pipe, a jagged piece of metal strapping tearing through his pants.

"Fuck dying. Fuck dying trapped in the walls of this fuck-infested fucking fuckbag island prison," he chanted, rhythmically working his ankle into a raw, bleeding frenzy. "Fuck you, too, you dirty rat. You dirrrrty raaat. Ha. Fuck giving my last will and testimonial and dying words to someone like you."

The rat in question, a sleek grey thing, perched on a pipe a few feet away, casually running its paws through its whiskers.

"I'm gonna eat ya. You give it time, you keep sniffin' around here, and I'm gonna just bite clean through your little stupid neck."

Easton Tucker had been burdened with the worst kind of sentence a man could get on Alcatraz. He was a clerical error. He didn't exist. He wouldn't be coming up for parole, and he wouldn't be eligible for any hearings, because somewhere across the country a man named Tucker Easton was serving out *his* twenty-five years in Leavenworth. Somehow, Easton Tucker and Tucker Easton were on the same bus for transfer, and Easton Tucker had slept through the entire thing. It was only when he stumbled off the transport bus to see a ship waiting in the bay that he realized something had gone wrong.

The past few months, he'd pleaded his case to anyone who'd listen, but the guards who did lend a friendly ear told him there was nothing they could do. *Patience*, that was the refrain. They were closing this joint soon, sending everyone back to dry land before this little rock eroded and crumbled into the sea. He didn't buy it, not a word. They loved to screw with your mind here, they loved to watch a glimmer of hope spark and fade.

Tucker knew the only boat that would carry him back across the water was one he built himself. To that end, he'd stolen six pairs of pants from the laundry and rolled them tightly into a knapsack that was lashed to his back with twine. He'd learned a trick back in the Navy, how to turn a pair of pants into a flotation device, and if one pair would hold a man up, surely six would convey him to safety posthaste.

But perhaps six had been too many, as the backpack was currently keeping him lodged between the two cinderblock walls of this narrow maintenance tunnel.

"How long you in for?" he asked the rat.

The rat scampered back three steps, then turned to continue staring at him.

"I'm not gonna squeal. I ain't asking for help."

He thought he'd add his name to the legends list with the Anglins and Morris, the ones who made it out. They were somewhere in the city by now, or rumbling through the hills nearby, stealing cars, drinking, screwing, dancing. The guards told everyone they didn't make it. Said they found chunks of their boat, a wallet, a paddle. They inspired a host of others to try, most recently Darl Parker and John Paul Scott. Parker messed up pretty good at the beginning and got caught, but Scott made it all the way to the Golden Gate. Yeah, he was half-dead and drowned, and they brought him back, but he proved it could be done.

Possibility, that's what Easton Tucker clung to.

He fumbled in his pocket for a blade, his favorite shiv crafted from the handle of a toothbrush. It was so finely sharpened on one side that he sometimes used it to shave. He swung his arm around to his chest and picked fitfully at the ropes that held his backpack. If he could get that off, he would have more room to work on getting his ankle free.

"How's about a hand here, pal?"

The rat blinked at him.

He tried to push higher with his free leg, but it was difficult to get any leverage on the slippery pipe. He could get about an inch of play before the metal strapping or screw or whatever it was down there bit back down into his ankle.

He pushed as high as the pain would let him, slipping his knife in and trying to saw through the rope on his shoulder. He fashioned the backpack straps out of braided shoelaces that he'd spent the past two weeks bartering for in the yard. Everyone had thought he was getting ready to end it.

"They're takin' us back to dry land. Whatcha wanna go hang yerself for anyway, ya scared o'water?" He muttered to himself as he worked, chanting everyone's disparaging words like a mantra to fuel his fire. He let out a small yelp as the shiv poked into his shoulder, drawing blood.

He repeated the phrase, *scared of water.* He wasn't scared of water; he was scared of bullets from the guard towers, or sharks. Water was nothing. Water he could handle. He didn't die when the Japs sank the *Indianapolis*, and he sure as hell wasn't worried about a little swim across the Bay.

The pipe beneath him emitted a sharp squeak, followed by a long, painful whine. He felt it vibrate, and assumed this is what happened whenever an inmate above flushed the john. The rattling moved the pipe enough that his ankle came free from whatever was stabbing it, but not far enough for his boot to scrape through to freedom.

Pain subsiding, he focused on the shoulder strap. The first one broke so quickly that he barked his knuckles against the wall, dropping the shiv. He slapped for it as it rattled down into the abyss below.

"You mind getting' that for me?" He asked the rat. "Do *somethin'*, would ya? Instead of staring at me with those beady eyes. I knew you were trouble. I knew it."

The rat lowered its body, flattening out against the pipe. It stared, nose wriggling.

He wouldn't need to cut through the other strap. Freeing one arm meant he could shimmy his body sideways away from the pack. With a couple of careful contortions, he felt it give behind him. It slid away to his right, and he hooked it with his elbow. Even with his eyes adjusted to the darkness, he couldn't figure out where to set it while he worked on the problem of his stuck foot.

Leaning forward, he discovered he could put pressure on the pipe and open up a little more space. The first time he did it, his boot snagged on the pipe and started to come off. Couldn't risk losing his shoes just yet. So he slowed down, exhaling, and pressed his toes into the pipe, inching his trapped leg higher, willing his boot to stay in place, ignoring the first two creaks that came from the pipe.

Another noise, like a dying cow, rang through the enclosed space. At first Tucker thought it was the voice of God himself, thunderous in the little tunnel, a deep bass note that sounded like a warning:

Nooooooooooooooooooo.

It was a death knell, a scream from metal that had been pushed beyond its limits.

Two giant blasts of sound came next, and the world started to list sideways, making his mind race back to that night his boat went down in WWII.

The pipe broke. Tucker felt his ankle break, as well, like he'd been shot, sending a pristine bolt of pain from his right big toe up into his left clavicle. The oddness of that new sensation took his mind off the fact that he was falling. What felt like minutes was probably seconds, and then more pain came.

One pop, his bad foot landing on concrete. Two pops, his head bouncing off the wall, ricocheting into the now-broken pipe (pop number three) before slamming down onto the ground.

He had enough time to register a sharp, hot stab in his right buttock before he began to drown.

Cold, slimy water vomited from the broken pipe that was now face-level, splattering his eyes, his ears. His right hand flopped dumbly behind him to find the source of the pain, and he knew two seconds before his fingers found it that it would be the handle of his trusty shiv, now lodged in his backside. He pulled it free and tried to stand, slipping and falling again. His adrenaline kicked in, and he found a way to flop over, push himself to all fours, and stand. The deluge that had been assaulting his face now pumped against his knees, slowly subsiding. He felt the back end of the pipe, twisted and folded, poking at his knees. When he turned, the old, rusted metal bit deep into the tendons there, plucking them like cheap nylon guitar strings until one frayed.

That singular note of agony was enough to bring the rest of senses back and make him realize what had happened. It was a small mercy that it was too dark to see, but the smell was unmistakable and overwhelming. It felt like the prison had been holding this in for all thirty of its years, that it had been constipated, and that maybe the guards were right, maybe it was shutting down. After all, didn't your bowels release at death?

Far away in the darkness, Easton Tucker heard a squeak.

"Rat!" He yelled. It was the only word he could find, the only syllable he could make, his sewage-spattered lips spraying his rage into the void. "Shit. House. Raaaaaat!"

He could only imagine what he looked like now. He tried to pretend it was only mud, that it would help conceal him once he got out of this place. He sniffled, instantly regretting that choice as a thick, viscous plug of sewage rocketed up into his nose and then back out as he choked.

If his momma could see him now. Easton Tucker had done a lot of things that wouldn't make her proud, most notable among them stabbing his momma through the heart with a broken mop handle. She was probably laughing at him from somewhere in Hell.

"I ain't supposed to be here!" He screamed. He bent down and hammered the broken pipe with his hand, a hollow booming that rang throughout the tight quarters. If someone was still on the island, they'd have heard it.

If.

His ankle was on fire. Every beat of his heart registered like a shotgun blast beneath his boot. He spent the next five minutes debating whether it would be better to keep his lips closed, risking the taste of shitwater, or keep his mouth open and head tipped forward, which seemed reasonable until he felt the tickle of water running down his cheeks and toward his mouth. He couldn't wipe at the muck with his encrusted hands, couldn't find the backpack to use some of the pants there to clean himself.

No two ways around it, Easton Tucker was going to have to eat shit today.

This was it. He was a ghost. Less than a ghost. If he died down here in this tunnel, nobody would know. On paper, Easton Tucker was safe and accounted for somewhere in Kansas. He had to get out. Had to see his wife again, even if just to piss on her grave.

He hobbled down the narrow crawlspace, pulling himself back up onto the remaining half of the pipe. If memory served, he'd only have about thirty feet to go before dropping down to an access panel that would let out somewhere just outside of the rec yard.

His ankle had gone numb, either from shock or the cold water or both. He reached the end of the pipe, his good foot losing traction. He skidded forward again, jamming his good toes between the pipe and the wall and smacking his face against the cinder blocks.

Behind him, the skittering of tiny rat feet.

"You my accomplice now?" Tucker spat, the taste of rotten eggs and rusty copper sluicing across his lips.

The rat said nothing.

He reached the end of the road, a faint light cutting through the wall near the access panel. He pushed against it. It gave way slowly at first, then popped free and clattered to the floor, echoing like a 21-gun salute.

Tucker pulled himself through the panel, leaving a large stain smeared across the tile floor. He rolled onto his back, wincing in pain. He'd tried. At least he'd tried. His ankle wouldn't hold up to any serious running, and there was still a fence to scale and a dive to the water. A swim with no flotation device.

"Fuck you, Darl and fuck you, John!" he shouted. "I'm here! I'm here, wherever the fuck this is!"

Darl Parker was apprehended on some nearby rocks in the bay. Tucker had befriended him as he recovered, and over the days, Parker told him the greatest secret he'd ever know.

Always have a backup plan.

Parker and Scott had gotten out using their Plan A, but Tucker learned that there was still an unused Plan B and C. They'd loosened some security bars here, opened some access panels there, and only Easton Tucker knew about them. This plan probably would have gone smoother with a partner, but loose lips sink ships. He worked for a few weeks to get the remaining necessities in place. He hadn't accounted for the shit storm he'd just survived.

Something about the thought of sinking ships coupled

with the smell he'd brought into the space made him lose his supper. And something about slinking through a narrow path brought on a second wave of intense nausea, and he lost the breakfast that had preceded his lunch. But he'd kept his meals light as the big day approached, to be as skinny as possible so he could slither through the narrow path to freedom. Small blessings.

He flopped away from his mess, pulling himself across the room until he came to a large steel table where he leveraged himself back to his feet.

He was somewhere in the lower levels of Building 64. He didn't know who'd designed the sewage systems for Alcatraz, but he thanked them for having a central access point to all of the island's buildings. None of the doors here would be locked. He had, at this point, *technically*, crawled his way to freedom. He could stop now. It made sense to give up. Every step he took sent more pain up his leg, he could barely breathe because of the stench he'd brought with him, and his only means of escape had been destroyed.

But his momma didn't raise a quitter, and that's the same thing he told her after the first few jabs with that mop handle didn't get the job done.

He didn't have anything waiting for him on the other side. Not a woman, not a job, not a safe place. But the sun was coming through the seam of the closed door to the room, and he had to know how it felt out there. He spied a mop leaning in the corner of the room and grabbed it, using it as a makeshift crutch. He hobbled forward, brazenly stepping through the door and out into the day, careless of who would see him.

Nobody was there. There was no clatter from the rec yard, no boats coming in, none of the supply trucks moving gear across the island. They had been telling him the truth. He waddled down a dirt path until he reached the wharf. The wind cut through him like a knife. Freedom felt like hell. He stared at the city lights across the Bay, as the rat skittered across his feet.

"What's escape, anyway? Gettin' away from the cops, right? Gettin' away from jail? I mean . . . I did it, right? Sort of? I'm the only one here. So it's sort of like I got away, right? Right?"

The rat stood on its hind paws and looked up at him. It checked over its shoulder and then scampered away across the rocks.

"I can't swim it," Tucker told the rat. "I can't."

The rat turned to face him.

"Die on the rocks or die in the water. You're not supposed to be here, that's the important thing," the rat said. "They're not coming back. They're never coming back."

Tucker stared at the rat in disbelief, his jaw hanging open. He blinked, a strange feeling at his temples as his sludge-encrusted skin dried in the open air.

"I'm covered in shit," he told the rat.

"You are," the rat agreed.

"Why didn't you talk before?"

"You've lost a lot of blood, Easton. You can't see it because your pants are filthy. Take them off."

Tucker hesitated, then nodded and did as he was told. Once, in the Navy, he'd been involved in an acid spill, a few splatters that ripped across his forearm and burned like the devil. As his pants slid down, that feeling returned to him, amplified tenfold as the fabric of his filthy pants peeled away from the skin on his leg.

He pawed at his right leg, massaging the back of his knee.

The rat tutted. "You shouldn't do that, your hands are disgusting."

Tucker ignored the rat, fingers probing at his leg. It felt distant and cold, made of rubber, but it was wet, even with the pants gone. The back of his knee hurt, and as he slid his hand up his thigh, his fingers probed the edges of a chasm that hadn't been there when he woke this morning.

He tried to test it, see how deep it went, but it stung, and he couldn't tell if it was the wound or his shit-stained fingers, so he eased back, walking his hands up the rim of this new geological feature. It started near the back of his knee, curling around to his inner thigh before taking another hard turn towards his rump.

"I really shanked myself, huh? God, that's deep. I need a doctor."

"You need a priest," the rat replied.

"What am I supposed to do now?"

"Confess? Sing. Sing your soul to me," the rat said.

Tucker swung a kick at the thing, but the strength went out of his leg and he collapsed in a heap. The side of his face bounced off the cement hard, and he felt his lips swell and his front teeth shift in a way that they hadn't since his last bar fight.

"I'm gonnn' die? Like thiff?"

He rolled onto his back and propped himself up on his elbows, looking at the ground. A perfect silhouette of his profile was painted in bile and blood. Swollen lips open in a silent scream, lines near the eye showing the grimace of pain.

"That's me!" Tucker said, jutting his chin at the ground.

"That's you. That's your whole life, Easton. That's everything you did and everything you'll ever be. That's as close to a memorial as you'll get, and it's more than you deserve." The rat scampered to Easton's feet and perched on its back paws, rubbing its forepaws together.

Tucker squinted at the rat. "You're not very nice."

"Neither were you."

"How can I make this right?"

The sky slowly began to shift, from a faded robin's egg blue to a brilliant white, then almost platinum. The world around Tucker went blurry.

"Confess to him," the rat said.

Tucker followed the rat's gaze to see a blurry shadow approaching. "Who's that?"

"Confess," the rat whispered.

Tucker tried to raise a hand to the shape. He'd never had much truck with angels or devils. Things were what they were and then they were done, but at this moment, he decided that it was probably best to make a good first impression.

"The only monument to sin is the stench we've left behind, and even that will be gone soon enough," the rat said.

"I'm sorry," Tucker said. "I'm sorry. I'm sorry, Momma. I'm sorry. I'm sorry about everything. I didn't even belong here. I never meant to—"

Thunder filled the sky, ripped through the heavens so hard that the sky warped. A blink later, Tucker felt a jolt of lightning strike his head. His right eye went near-blind, and his left exploded from his temple, riding a wave of bone and blood and brain, spattering across the silhouette he'd created moments earlier.

Was this death?

He blinked, his vision resolving until there was only light and that dark blue monstrosity towering over him that resolved into familiar shapes: arms, legs, a service revolver, a badge on its chest shining brighter than the golden morning sun. Indistinct voices came to him in the light, from far away. Then more shadows joined the first one, and that chorus grew.

Who are you?

Easton felt his cheek growing cold in the shallow puddle of sewage and blood and bone he'd created, his monument, and though he could no longer speak, he finally knew the answer to that question.

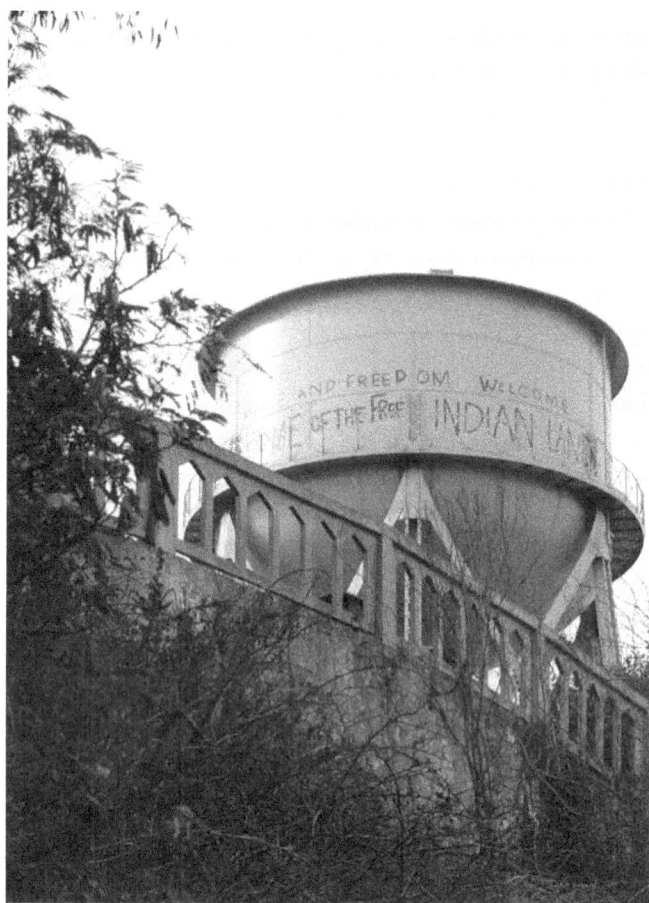

Xystocheir

Carrie Laben

"Hey, I'm sorry about your dog, man."

Bob says it for the third time, not that Wyatt is trying to count. He's decided to stop holding Bob's weird tics and forced joviality against him at least for tonight. But the last thing he needs right now is reminders about Falcon, or the sons of bitches who'd killed her. That's why he's here. It's not like he's going to *forget*.

"I really am, dude. I mean it. Whoever did that, shit, they deserve to get the same done to them. If it was me, I'd saw their heads right off slow. Dull knife."

There's a real risk that a shoulder poke is coming next, a demand to be acknowledged, especially in the dark where Bob can't tell if Wyatt is looking at him or not, whether he's appreciating the bravado and shock value of the statement. A shoulder poke on another night would turn Wyatt around, make him tell Bob to get someone younger and dumber to help out with his big-shot schemes, get him back in his kayak. He couldn't bear to trust his life to Bob's half-assed navigation. Point his compass towards home where he could crack a beer and sit on the back steps, listening to

91

the killdeers cry until dawn, with no one around but silent, straightforward Falcon. Not tonight. Never again.

"This is the next spot," he says quietly instead. Whole damn thing is Bob's idea anyway. Maybe Bob could shut up and do some of the damn work. And then Wyatt thinks, *no, you're doing it again.* Bob isn't in front. Bob isn't reading the map. But that's because you're the one who knows the island. Bob is lugging the paint cans. And Bob paid for the paint. Bob has paid for car repairs and flophouses and bail and an unending stream of mushroom pizzas for damn near everyone in the group. And Bob actually wants people to come together and do things, in a movement where the biggest heroes are men and . . . well, mostly men who wander off into the wilderness alone to nurse their cranky-bastard ways in the bits of forest or desert or mountain that have been spared. Which Wyatt himself would do, if he had his way.

He's not fancy enough to think of himself as a philosopher though—just an entomologist, and not even that with his ABD—so wandering off in the middle of a hundred-year environmental emergency would be self-indulgent. You don't do that.

Before Bob can start talking again, Wyatt gestures with the flashlight, kept low and invisible from a distance, at a rock that glitters with flecks of quartz. Bob pulls out his brush and daubs paint across the top. In the daylight, it'll just look like a splash of guano from any distance. Wyatt pulls out the other light, the black light, and steps back to take the point of view of a stranger—maybe Beth, with the little limp that's a legacy from her old man, or Eddie, who though he'll never admit it gets spooky in the dark—and makes sure the glow of the paint will be easy to spot. Once the strike team lands, they'll want to move quickly and efficiently to the "high-value targets." Bob's exact words. A fancy term for a bunch of old buildings full of mostly bad memories. Although it'll be a shame that they'll lose the graffiti that the Indians left behind.

"Okay, dude, looks good, onward and upward." Bob's in a hurry like always, gung ho. What Wyatt's uncles would have called, approvingly, a go-getter. Not the "wander off into the woods or the desert or the mountains" type at all. Focused on a goal like a moth on a pheromone trail, when to be honest most of the rest of the group had been circling the porch light. Wyatt himself hadn't taken things as seriously as he could've, he realizes as he scrambles up the rocky trail, almost seeing Falcon's tail wagging up ahead. At 27, he was (horribly enough) the grown-up in the room at so many meetings, and he's always used that to advocate caution, peace, nonviolence. Until Bob came along. He didn't want to be the guy who got people going nuts and getting killed. But someone got killed anyway, the person—and she was a person, even if she wasn't a human—who had the least say in it at all. There's no other reason for anyone to kill her besides the activism, and he's had threats before, but he honestly didn't think anyone could have gotten to her so fast and so quietly.

He'd still rather be out on the flotilla next week with the Peace Navy than doing this. The whole thing where he helps map out the action and then stays back at Eddie's apartment waiting to provide "support," "logistics," or whatever fancy word Bob comes up with this time for listening to the news on the radio. It's just a fig leaf, a childish one, something that's supposed to make him feel involved but safe. If someone gets killed, or hurt, it's on him as much as anyone else. He'd always thought that was a line he wouldn't cross, until he walked out into the back yard Wednesday morning to see why Falcon hadn't scratched at the door to come back inside. And even now, it's hard to keep the fury burning in his mind if he remembers it's not just the faceless bastards who did this thing who could suffer, but Eddie or Beth or, hell, even Bob. Maybe he doesn't have the passion. Maybe the urge for vengeance just isn't in him, even though it's not just a lost, murdered blue merle cattle dog at risk, but every fish and bird that uses the Bay, the ecosystem out beyond, the whales everyone loves, even the tiny crustaceans that no one knows. When you think of what's at stake, maybe there's something wrong with him that a murderous urge isn't burning all the time.

Wyatt's steps go wrong while he's thinking this, and he stumbles on a rock. Bob runs into the back of him, banging a bucket inside the curve of his knee hard enough to bring him all the way down. Paint sloshes onto Wyatt's jeans.

"Dammit!"

It's sharp, but it's only a whisper. Wyatt never enjoyed disturbing the quiet dark. Bob backs up a few steps, leaving the cans on the ground and hands high in a placating gesture. The actual words "I'm sorry" aren't in his vocabulary, but he can manage "Well, shit" and an abashed face for a few seconds. Wyatt, still on the ground, rolls into a sitting position and raises the wrong light to inspect the damage. Instead of blood or, as he hopes, merely dirt on his knee, he sees glowing spatters everywhere. One of these long smears on the ground darts away to shelter beneath an overhang of greywacke.

Wyatt's mind switches modes instantly, and he scoots towards the vanishing glow, no longer worried about blood.

He catches a glimpse of a tail disappearing, and now that his eyes know what they're seeking, the pattern is instantly recognizable.

A millipede, *Xystocheir dissecta dissecta*. He's heard that their cousins on the mainland fluoresce, too, but no one had ever thought to check out these guys. If he hadn't dropped out of grad school, he could have gotten a hell of a paper out of this.

There are six or eight of the little bastards, all glowing a fine pale-blue, short laceworks of legs fringing their bodies. He has a moment imagining describing all this to Falcon, explaining everything while she cocks her head at such a strange, unearthly light.

"Come on, dude."

This time Bob does poke him, twice, and Wyatt has no idea how long he's been staring, and he doesn't really care. Can't the man *see*? He pushes the hand away from his shoulder.

"Man, are you pussing out on me?" Bob's voice raises uncomfortably over the dull splash of the waves. "What are you doing? Don't you be pussing out on me now, you asshole. I should've known you didn't have the balls for this."

Wyatt reaches in and manages to snatch up three scrambling millipedes with one hand. Some old skills never leave. "Look at these." He tries to shine the blacklight on them, but it's an awkward angle and they're still trying to crawl away.

"Okay, we got paint on some bugs," Bob says. "That's weird and all but . . . are you high? Did you come out here high? You're going to fuck everything up."

Wyatt shakes his head. "This is a genus of millipede found in California and nowhere else in the world. This is *exactly* the kind of thing we're fighting for. Take a minute and appreciate them, for Christ's sake, and let me rest my leg."

It's stupid to try to explain anything to Bob, and it's ruining the moment, but Wyatt is stubborn sometimes. He holds the millipedes out, still expecting to share an epiphany.

This pisses Bob off even more.

"Fine. Stare at bugs. I'm not the guy who found his dog hanging in a tree with its muzzle taped shut and its fucking feet cut off. I'd think you'd care more about that, you gutless wonder."

Wyatt stares down at his handful of *Xystocheir*, their antenna wagging gently as they realize there's nowhere to go. "You know," he says slowly, trying to sound higher than he'd ever been, "the Indians, when they were here during their occupation of Alcatraz from 1969 to 1971, they used these guys for a ceremony. To prove their bravery before the big confrontations and whatnot."

Bob will believe any goddamn thing is an old Indian ceremony, Wyatt's hoping.

"Prove your bravery by goddamn getting up and walking." Bob says, moving as if to slap the millipedes out of Wyatt's hand. But Wyatt's too fast.

"Scared?" Wyatt says, inflecting the word the way his uncles might have, but maybe more stoned. Slower. As though he's prepared to sit here and be obtuse all night long, staring at the man who knew the painful details of his dog's death, details Wyatt hadn't told anyone.

"Scared of what?"

"Eating the millipedes. The Indians did it. It's not so complicated. It just shows you're part of the food chain."

Sorry about this, he thinks to the creatures in his palm, and then he raises his hand to his mouth. It's an old party trick all magicians and entomologists learn to impress the kiddies, chewing theatrically and dropping one lucky millipede behind him.

He holds out his hand, the two less-fortunate millipedes still caged by his sweaty fingers.

"Your turn."

Bob stares at him hard, then reaches out and plucks the smallest millipede up, pops it into his mouth, and crunches fast, wincing. Wyatt waits for a retch, but to Bob's credit he gulps it down fast, then picks up the paint cans with a flourish, as if he'd really just conquered an ancient ceremony of great meaning.

"Okay," he says, calmer now, "can we go?"

"Sure," Wyatt says, lurching to his feet, energized. "We've only got a bit before it kicks in, so we'd better get as much done as we can."

"Kicks in?"

"The cyanide. That's why they glow, you dig? To warn predators they're loaded full of poison."

"Jesus Christ!" Both buckets fall with a clatter, long streaks of paint running like insects and soaking into the sandstone all around them.

Bob would have been a shitty Indian, Wyatt thinks with satisfaction.

"Some of them have a dose that will kill a man," he says. "Others, not quite. That's where the bravery comes into play."

Ten seconds' thought would reveal the holes in that story, but with any luck at all, Bob's past thinking about anything any time soon.

"You insane bastard," Bob marvels. "Why would you do that to me?"

"You think we don't know a rat when we see one?" Wyatt asks him, ashamed that, in fact, they hadn't. "You show up from nowhere. You know no one. You have all sorts of money and no job." He pauses, wonders what other tells they missed early on. "You only ever want to do the glory-hound stuff: arson, guns, fighting with cops. No organizing, no building connections, not even nice, low-key trespassing or civil disobedience. Always the tough-guy bullshit."

"The hell I am!" Bob's feeling it already though, slumping downwards along the steep part of the trail, back hunched, not unlike a rat at all.

"You don't know the first fucking thing about the environment, to be honest. You don't know the difference between a millipede wearing graffiti and one that glows on its own."

"You ate one, too!" He's far below Wyatt on the trail now.

"Yep, too late for me. You got me, like you got Falcon. But if we both die out here, the others will know something went wrong, and they won't fall into whatever trap you and the pigs had set up for us."

Bob runs, and Wyatt watches him go. He'll go for his boat and try to get to medical help across San Francisco Bay, sweating his brains out all the way. And he'll either make it or be swept out to sea. But he won't get where he's going as fast as Wyatt can kayak home. Not with this tide. There'll be time to warn the others.

There's a skitter of rocks. A thump and a scream. A splash. Wyatt thinks, *that really wasn't as bad as I expected.*

Then he thinks about how the millipedes with cyanide are the *Motiyxia* and not the *Xystocheir,* and the fact that they lived nowhere near the island is a pretty thin fig leaf, even compared to Bob's plan. He's killed a man. He finds it hard to care.

He'll have to leave, since he'd been the last one to see Bob alive, head for the forest or the desert or the mountains that have been spared. He'll tell the others to go join the flotilla and stop the dumping if they can. The rain and wind would wear away their paint, eventually, and even the unlucky millipede would be replaced by a newly hatched nymph soon enough. He'd find someone to describe the glow to again, someday. Maybe another cattle dog.

The Eighth

by Johnny Shaw

I kept my promise. If I didn't keep my word, who was I as a wife and a Christian? For all my sins, I would never forget that I held his life in my hands. He loved me and trusted me with what little hope he had left. In a place with no reason for hope, that was everything.

Every eighth of the month for the last six years, I took the journey to see my husband in whatever penitentiary currently housed him. Except when the eighth fell on a weekend, then it was the first Monday after.

As Harold moved across the country, I moved with him. Once I picked up and moved from my hometown, it wasn't anything to do. I wasn't leaving anything, my roots already severed. I became accustomed to starting in a new town, a new home, and a new life. Eight moves total. Indiana, Illinois, Kansas, and for the last sixteen months, San Francisco. The final stop, one which we spent both together and apart.

Our journey together would end here.

My monthly ritual on visiting days was not unpleasant. I considered myself a happy person, but on those days I had given up trying to control my feelings. I usually settled on somber as a more appropriate mood. Not glum, but stoic. Inside, I could find peace in the repetition, if not joy. During the rest of the month, my routine made it easy to forget that my husband was only two miles away. But on the eighth, I received the perennial reminder of the strangeness of that reality.

One visit per month by permission of the warden. That was all that was allowed. What harm would it have done for me to see him more than that? Twice, even? Was it a part of his punishment, or were they worried we would plan an escape, if we only had more time? Or was it just laziness? Fewer visits meant less work. I'd been in enough prisons to know that the rules were rarely developed with the prisoners in mind. Feckless administrators with uncreative solutions to problems that didn't exist.

I left my small house at first light and walked through the low mist that filled the streets. I never ate breakfast, settling for the luxury of two cigarettes on the short walk. I found different routes, but always ended up in the same place. The coldest place in the city. The pier. With the wind from the bay cutting through my coat, I waited with a small group of men. Some of the faces were familiar, others new to me. Three men in uniforms, two men in dark suits, and another man carrying a black medical bag. Guards, lawyers, and a doctor or dentist. Men commuting to work. I was the only one boarding to visit a prisoner.

The ferry pointlessly arrived on time. I suppose I should admire the ferryman's punctuality, but never had anybody been in less of a hurry than the people going to or from Alcatraz Island.

The Eighth

Women and children disembarked from the small boat. The wives and children of the guards who lived on Alcatraz heading into the city to do their weekly shopping or to attend school. They gave me knowing looks, eyes full of pity or spite.

I boarded with the men, nodding to the ferryman. He knew me by sight, nodded back. We hadn't exchanged a word to each other in at least half a year. What was there to say?

I found a seat. The other passengers and I rode in silence as the ferry chopped through the Bay toward Alcatraz. The trip never took more than fifteen minutes, but every second held a moment. I no longer looked back at the city. Even our most recent past is our past. I kept my eyes on the rocky island as it approached. That was my present and future.

By the time we reached the opposite pier, my cheeks were wet with tears. The men on the boat looked away, assuming that I was crying, not that I was sensitive to the diesel fumes and salt water. I had finished doing all my crying a long time ago. Dabbing at the corner of my eyes with my handkerchief, I did my best to avoid smearing my makeup. I wanted to look my best for Harold.

I stepped off the boat. No hand from the ferryman or the guards that waited on the dock. They consulted their paperwork, grunted commands, and pointed me where I already knew to go. They never once looked me in the eyes. I never took it as insult, but instinct. These were men who were paid to oversee the imprisoned. If they were like me, they had been taught in church to treat all men the same. Here they had been taught to treat these men differently. That forced them to treat everyone different.

Nobody was born a prison guard. They had to learn how

to perform their role. As I had learned to be a prison widow. Nobody taught me how to be married to a man serving a 99-year sentence.

Through the repetition of processing my visitation, I was treated like a stranger. Faces I saw monthly asked the same questions. I filled out the same forms, identically except for the year. With two guards to accompany me, we walked through one building, outside to another, and down a long hallway into the visiting room.

Save for the guard that monitored the visit, I was alone in the spare room. Four windows of thick glass, each with an intercommunication device that I would use to interact with my husband. No chance of physical contact. The salt air had rusted the exposed corners of the chipped counter. Some of the pea green paint peeled to reveal gray.

I waited for Harold, sitting on the backless stool. I glanced at the guard who would listen to every word that we spoke to each other. Another rule. So many rules. Harold wasn't even allowed to talk about his life in the prison. Which gave him very little to talk about it.

It meant that I did most of the talking.

Harold gave me the smile that had made me fall in love with him. Like he was thinking of a joke, but it was only for him. He looked at me like a husband should. He made me feel beautiful, desired, and loved, even in the dank surroundings.

Harold seemed to have aged another year in the month that I'd seen him. A few more lines, thicker bags under his eyes, his hair thinning in the middle.

"You look well," I said.

"Not as good as you, baby. You're beautiful as ever."

"The California air suits me."

"I told you I'd take you to see the West Coast."

I laughed, not the first time he'd told that joke.

"You don't miss home."

"This is home now."

"Not too cold for you?" he asked

"No snow. I don't miss the snow."

"But it's colder here, you know? Illinois, Indiana, Kansas, even Minnesota, those were places where the cold made sense. Here, I don't know. Maybe it's just here inside, but some days I feel like I can't ever get warm. Like I ain't never going to be warm again."

"I might be able to buy a coat for you. I can write a request to Warden Swope."

"Save your money. I have a good coat. Good enough. I just feel like complaining." Harold tried to smile again, but he couldn't hear the joke. "The cold is just colder."

"Are you sleeping? You look tired."

"Better. What else is there to do?"

"Are you reading your Bible?"

"Every night, baby."

We told each other what we wanted to hear, an unspoken agreement. Lies and truth didn't matter. The words didn't matter. We were never going to be in the same room together. I would never touch the man I married again. Why fight? Why bring conflict to the brief purgatory we had? Our marriage was already separated by steel and concrete and men in uniforms and the entire San Francisco Bay.

The silences were the hardest. There were always silences. It felt like a personal failure to let even the most mundane conversation ebb. As much as I prepared myself to have things to talk about, I got lost in the discomfort of it all. I limited myself to certain topics. I didn't want to talk about things that he would never have again. He would never walk in a park, eat an ice cream cone, or travel farther than three hundred yards from where he sat.

I was sure he thought about those things, but we never talked about them. We didn't have to. I could see his hope dying with each visit. It aged him, slowly killing him. To take away a man's life is just for the crimes committed, but to take a man's hope was cruel and unnecessary.

While Harold maintained his innocence to the world, I knew that he belonged in prison. He had robbed that mail truck. He had killed those two men. And he had escaped from prison three times. He could not take back his actions. The most he could do was fulfill his agreement with society and atone for his sins. That meant living the rest of his life on this island. He would die here. Then he would answer to God. As we all do. As I would as well.

I wasn't sure where I stood with God. Harold had never told me what he did to make his money, but I knew he was doing something besides the lies he told me. Daddy had told me that he had heard stories, that Harold had a reputation. He had warned me that Harold was a bad man.

If he was bad, I didn't fall in love with his badness. He was nothing but good to me. Bad men aren't bad to everyone, and bad men don't only do bad things. Even now, it's hard to see the man that took the lives of those other men. I only saw my Harold.

"How's our boy?" Harold asked.

"Still with my parents," I said. "I haven't heard from them since the last time we spoke, but I'm sure they're taking good care of him."

"Wish I could see him. I miss him."

"He misses you, I'm sure."

"How long you been working at that place?"

"Five months."

"You like it?"

"The work is good. The pay is fair. There have been changes in the typing pool. They had to let some girls go."

He nodded and looked away. It sounded like I was complaining. The fact that I worked was failure enough to him. That I showed any sense of disappointment in the job was even worse. I had to watch my words. I changed the subject.

"Do you want to pray with me?" I asked.

"You pray. I'll watch. I don't think God much cares about me right now."

"Of course He cares."

"I like watching you pray."

I lowered my head and prayed softly for God to look after Harold, our son, our parents, and the rest of our family, though Harold's kin no longer spoke to us. I prayed to make Harold's circumstances as pleasant as possible. To remind God that despite his sins, he was serving his punishment here on earth. To make the difficult days bearable. I could feel Harold's eyes on me.

"Amen," I said.

"Amen," he repeated.

The guard stood up from his desk, the chair screeching on the concrete. I turned with a jump. He shrugged and motioned toward the door. It was time.

"I love you, Harold," I said. "And remember, God loves you."

"Just so long as you do," he said. "See you next month, baby."

* * *

A guard appeared behind Harold. I watched them guide my husband back into the mysterious bowels of the building. I imagined a prison cell like I'd seen in the movies. Small, uncomfortable, bare. I didn't wish for my husband to be executed, but I didn't see how 99 years of waiting was more humane. He didn't look like he would make it another five. Twenty-eight years old and already an old man.

The ferry ride back to the city always felt shorter. The buildings growing larger as we approached the pier. Difficult to deny their beauty.

Back on the pier before noon, I continued my monthly ritual. My feet still unsteady from the ferry, I walked through the city. After an hour of aimless wandering, I found my way to a street-corner peddler selling flowers. He made the loveliest bouquets and greeted me with a toothless smile. I found the nearest taxi stand, and with the money I saved throughout the month, I hired a car to take me to Colma.

I knew it was wrong to keep Jason's death from Harold. The fever had taken him so quickly. Alive and mischievous one day, sick the next, and gone forever one day later. Once, I wrote a note to send to the prison, but threw it away. I went on my regular monthly visit two weeks after, but never found the courage to tell him. I could only see the pain it would cause, the hope it would take away. I couldn't find a good reason to tell him other than it was the truth. That wasn't good enough.

My only lie was in the not telling. Jason was surely in Heaven with my parents. They had died last year. Another loss that I never saw the need to relay to Harold.

The Eighth

It was always strange that the cemetery was so much warmer than the city. I walked down the familiar trail and found Jason's grave. I set half the flowers on the small stone, saving the other half for my kitchen. I liked the small comfort in knowing that we were sharing their beauty. I sat for hours, talking to Jason and praying to God.

When the sky dimmed, I stood and walked through the graves out of the cemetery. Until next month. And the next.

Bodhisattva Badass
by Mark Rapacz

Part I: You's a Bitch

The year is 1932, and you're a prisoner, bitch. You were thrown onto a steam train and forced to ride many miles from your hometown in Nebraska to a place you only know as "The Rock."

You're blindfolded, and you've suffered severe beatings from the prison guards who only answer to The Man. You have a friend, though, and his name is Jimmy. You met him at the train station's Prisoner Processing Room. You've been praying in your cattle car since it left Nebraska and traveled over the terribly cold Rocky Mountains and descended into the sweltering heat of the California high deserts. First you were freezing, then you couldn't breathe from the heat and stench of the future prisoners all around you pissing, crapping, sweating, and bleeding on each other. None of you know why you've been captured, but you're pretty sure it has something to do with your criminal activities. You did kill that bank clerk during a badass robbery.

The stink is overwhelming, and you're so jam-packed in that cattle car all you hear are rumors from your buddy

Jimmy—who also killed a bank clerk—that you're heading to a place you've only heard foretold in ancient ass-kicking legends.

The Rock. Alcatraz. The Big Apple's Clink. It goes by many unsavory names.

And you're like, "Oh, shit, motherfucker. Shit's 'bout to get real, dawg. And to think I was just a farm boy who got caught up in a bank robbery, and I ain't even was the triggerman."

And Jimmy just looks at you dead to rights, and he laughs a big, booming laugh that makes everybody in the cattle car shut the fuck up.

"Ain't none of us triggermen, son. We all just bitches to the The Man."

And everybody lets that sink in for a while because truer words have never been spoken to a gathering of the most Free Thugs Alive. And during this time of reflection, all's completely fucking quiet for a long-ass time, except for the dude who was just shanked with a big-ass splinter torn off the boxcar—oh, and those rabid rats feeding on his guts.

You don't know what to say to Jimmy. Ain't nobody knows what to say because you're really all just bitches to The Man. But the thing is, this cattle car ride through the California High Desert is going to forever be branded into your memory as the last time serving Hard Time at the Big Time wasn't so bad.

Because every man in that car was the baddest motherfucker in his hometown, sure, and every one of them killed a bank clerk.

But now, son, you're all just whiny little bitches about to be digested by a monster we in the United States of America know as the Federal Penitentiary System.

Part II: You's a Badass

The year is 1937, and now you, The Kid, and your buddy
Jimmy have been doing hard time for five years. You've
been getting jacked, lifting weights, eating food, and
doing push-ups and general health-conscious calisthenics.
You've become total supreme badasses of the penitentiary.
When you and Jimmy swagger down Broadway, everybody
shuts the fuck up, even the guards. Just being around you,
dudes piss their black and whites. Things are getting
pretty fucking awesome for you and Jimmy. You are kings
of this joint, and you don't want this dream to ever end.
The whole world is your bitch.

And sometimes there are days where you and Jimmy
have to set aside your noble Ways of Peace and be total
badasses and royally fuck dudes up in the mess room if
they talk back. For instance, you often stab men in the neck
with a fork, but they deserve the fuck out of it for being
less enlightened than you. Other days, you and Jimmy are
totally benevolent Bodhisattvas turning a place that is the
very definition of Hell into something that is almost like
the Calm of the Forever Astral Grace. For instance, the day
Jimmy announced the following words in the Rec Yard,
while the forlorn cries of seagulls echoed overhead and
steam boats groaned on the distant waves:

"All right, all you Thugs and Badasses, gather around
these stone bleachers!" Jimmy shouted louder than usual,
to drown out a biplane overhead. "I decree there ain't going
to be no more stabbing each other in the neck with forks
or mutilating each other while we sleep or killing the new
meat for sport. We may be criminals to that world out there,

but in here we are free men if we want to be. We don't have to make this such a bitch for each other. We can make a peaceful place, not just a place of badasses and bitches."

And the Rec Yard roared that day, and you, The Kid did, too, because there were a lot of dudes out there who didn't want to be assaulted anymore. And Jimmy had to make everyone pipe the fuck down as he carried on.

"Also, some of you have found covert partners here to shack up with. I may have killed a lot of women and children, but I know true love when I see it. I know a lot of you men have true loves here today listening to these words. So I think that's okay."

And the men were embarrassed at first because it went against their old-fashioned 1930s ideas of marriage and love, but then they looked into their hearts and knew that good men should like other good men and receive no judgment.

Then, suddenly, the prison guards came, and with them was a man named Clarence Rex, who was as dumb as they come and believed in those outdated biblical values and ruled his roost with ideas forged in the Middle Ages.

"What's this I hear about you and non-Christian ideals of love?" he asked, jabbing a fat finger in Jimmy's chest.

Jimmy got right in his face and said, "I, as a straight, badass motherfucker, said all men should be free to love whomever they want and do what the fuck they want."

And then Jimmy took his huge fist and swung right into Clarence Rex's face, killing him dead instantly. Everyone stood horrified for a moment, until the horde of guards swarmed them. First thing they did was make an example out of Jimmy, the new Savior of the Yard. They shot him exactly thirty-three times in his pelvic region, then twice in the head. It was gruesome, and you still ponder the significance of that number.

After that, a riot broke out in honor of Jimmy's Decree. Many brave men died that day, while you, The Kid, ended up in solitary just for being such a badass. And you spent the next seven years remembering Jimmy's words about freedom and justice and love and hope and compassion, and that's all you thought about as you planned your amazing escape and revenge.

Part III: You's a Bodhisattva (but still a Badass)

You've been in The Hole for probably like ten years now, but you haven't been wasting your time. You've continued your exercise regime to an obsessive degree. It's all you do. It's become your religion, your path to Enlightenment. With every push-up, you think one thing:

Get the fuck out.

You also think another thing:

Remember what Jimmy decreed.

So each time the guard comes around and lets in that precious moment of light when he drops a plate of gruel through your slot, you lick your chops, not because you want to eat the food they surely pissed in, but because you can taste that little bit of sunshine. You taste revenge and freedom, fried to perfection on our nearest star, and it tastes like Taco John's classic Super Potato Olés®. Meaning delicious as fuck.

What the guards don't know, and what you never let on, is that you've been spending each day carefully toughening up your fingernails and doing a special finger exercise you learned in a dream about Yoga Jesus. And it's taken years and years of hellish shit to become hard as adamantium and strong as a neutron blast. Anthropomorphized.

And more than once you thought about killing yourself. Hell, by year five in The Hole, and with triple finger workouts every day, all you'd have to do is flick yourself right in the Adam's apple and you'd be sleeping with those petunias made out of Alcatraz concrete made from the calcified remains of the shellfish in the Bay below.

In fact, one day you were about to do it. Had your finger cocked at your throat until the guard comes by, opens the slot, drops the gruel in, and says, "You whore-bitch of a man, hope you choke on this shit today so I don't have to see you tomorrow," like always.

And you're about to release your trigger finger, crushing that little neck bone, but you're just thinking, "That's the last fucking time The Man says that shit. I'm making his bitchass wish come true."

So, you, The Kid with your Hindi-level asceticisms and ninja-like abilities to meditate all the damn time (because there's jack else to do in the dark), decide to put your super hands to super use.

You step to the toilet and grip it. The porcelain is cool, and you just squeeze the living fuck out of it, and it crumbles like really brittle dry putty in your hands. You whisper to yourself, "That was for Jimmy, but this next shit is for me," and you clear the porcelain debris and just start pulling the copperworks right out of the concrete with your amazingly sculpted fingers, hands, forearms—hell, your whole body is shredded like no other, and you're just tearing the guts out of this Concrete Beast so savagely you almost feel bad for it.

Soon enough, there's a man-sized hole in the floor of your cell, and you drop down it, right into the middle of the guards' mess hall. You look around calm as fuck and say with an awesome smile, "Ain't no slop time, bitches," and you beat the piss out of all of them and get the keys to the front door.

You walk up to that giant steel-riveted door, and you slip in the skeleton key, and you push those two-ton doors open like a man who's never been more alive in his life.

Because you haven't till that day. And with the sun shining on the water, you know you're about do something nobody has ever done, ever: Escape The Rock and live...

Which you do! Only to become president of Venezuela where you rule as a Benevolent Dictator until the end of days. You're beloved by its citizens for your charity and intelligence and remembered as the only leader to nationalize health care so damn quick, create a school system that produces the smartest badass Latin American kids the world has ever seen, and eliminate poverty completely through genius social welfare programs. But that's not all: you sent a secret manned space mission to Mars, invented the Internet, and discovered a sustainable energy source (Hint: it's nuclear fusion) that you won't reveal to the world until they can prove they can handle it responsibly, since you know from your time in Alcatraz—where you learned all your guiding principles—that with great fucking power comes great fucking responsibility.

Your only regret is that though you come close to creating an Eden on Earth, you are unable to properly forgive yourself for not going out of your way to forgive your father, who was the one who really killed that Nebraskan bank clerk so many years ago. But so goes the cycle of renewal and rebirth, as you all stumble toward Nirvana, perfection forever just out of reach of your wretched but muscular hands.

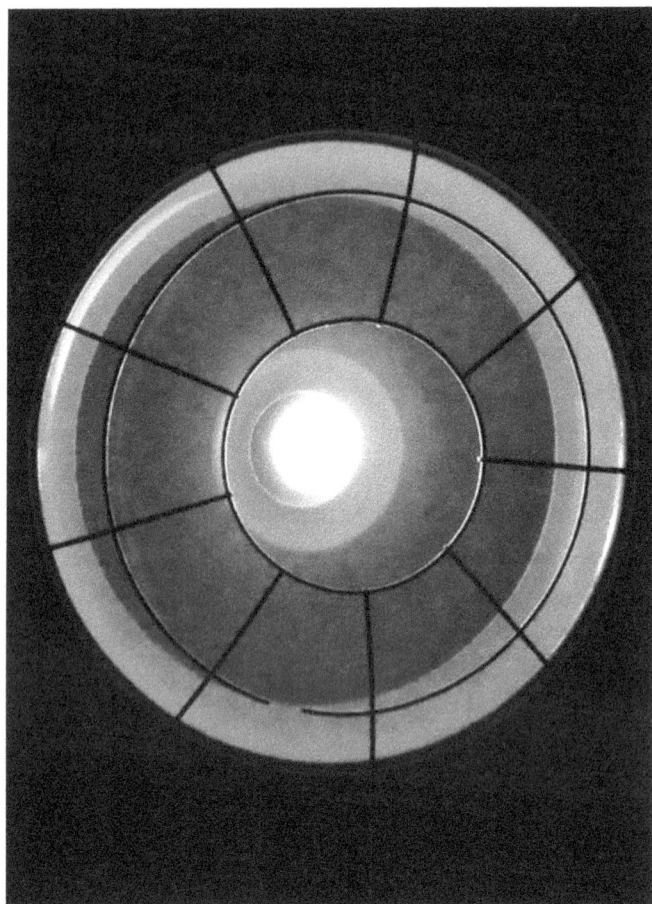

The Ghosts of 14D
by Joshua Chaplinsky

As I raised the Spirit Box to the food slot, Alcatraz lived up to its reputation as one of the most haunted places on Earth . . .

"Who are you?" Todd said into the darkness. It was more a command than a question. "What's your name?"

Danny peaked out from behind the camera. For a split second, his brain continued to render what he saw in night vision, then everything went black. He held his breath and listened. Counted off the seconds in his head.

Somewhere around twelve, the box spit static. The word *name* popped up on the digital display.

"Name," the box said out loud. Its robotic voice reverberated across the empty cell block.

Name! The intake guard barked.
Six-thirty.
Ante or Post Meridiem?
Post, sir.
Time zone?
Uh . . .

119

The guard looked up from his form.

Time zone?

I . . . don't know, sir.

What do you mean, you don't know?

I . . .

The guard jerked his pen over his shoulder.

Over there, with the rest of the GMTs.

But I—

Next!

Six-thirty shuffled off to the left, where he waited in line to be hosed down and deloused.

Name!

"Dude, did you hear that?" Todd slapped Danny's arm.

"All it did was repeat you."

"Yeah, but there was something else. You didn't feel it?" He whipped out an EDI meter and stuck it through the slot. The numeric display took a nosedive. "It's almost ten degrees cooler in there."

"Temperature doesn't translate to good TV."

Todd glared at his cameraman. "But being a dick does?"

Danny shrugged.

"It'll be fine," Todd said. "I'll add some voiceover in post." He fiddled with a dial.

"Ask him if he knew the Birdman!"

"Shut up."

I awake naked in the hole. I know I'm awake because my eyes are open, not that it makes much difference. I scan the darkness, as if I can see through it. Despite the crushing loneliness, it always feels like someone is watching me.

I roll into a sitting position and lean my back against the wall. Something scurries across my shoulder, but I ignore it. Of all the days to relive, why does it always have to be that one? I know I'll never get out of this place, but the thought of another hard reset terrifies me more than anything. To go back to those initial moments . . .

I can't think of anything worse. Not even the events that put me here, which rarely cross my mind these days.

You're hurting me . . . I can't breathe . . .

I sleep as little as possible. I stay up nights and listen to the icy water of the Bay crashing against stone, wind battering the walls around me. Some nights, the wind carries voices with it. The Indians on watch talking softly or singing a traditional song. Something about overflowing rivers and the end of the world. Something about the evils of the moon. It's almost as if they're singing about this place.

"You think we're making a difference?" I hear one of them say.

"I don't know," says another. "I'm going back to school come September."

I rarely, if ever, converse with the other inmates. Thick walls and asshole screws make sure of that. Most times, the hallways are empty, but on occasion they fill with the shuffling of feet as throngs of gawkers are given a private look at where the animals sleep. Or is it slept? But mostly they just echo with the sound of their own emptiness.

Six-thirty circled the yard, trying to find a spot along the perimeter to post up.

What're you in for? A fellow inmate asked. He scratched at his arm, leaving a series of white lines.

I hurt someone.

Naw, man. You're supposed to say you're innocent. We're all innocent!

It was an accident . . .

Not the same thing. Trust me.

Six-thirty stared at a loose stitch on the inmate's jumpsuit. The man's shadow circled them both as the sun crossed the sky.

No, really, what're you—

The inmate suddenly made a sound like air escaping a tire. Six-thirty watched another man withdraw a long, thin piece of metal from the inmate's side. Seconds poured out of the tiny puncture wound. He hadn't even seen the assailant approach, and already the man had moved on, like a spirit. Dropped the shiv at Six-thirty's feet. It earned him his first stint in the hole.

Back in the '40s, before it became my permanent home, they say a man went crazy in 14D. Screamed all night about there being someone in the cell with him. A pair of eyes watching from the corner, reflecting the light.

Of course the screws ignored him, taunted him, even. Eventually, they got bored and went up to the roof for a smoke. And when they went back to look in on him early the next morning, they found him strangled, rats already chewing at his tongue.

Probably just a mess-hall tale used to scare new fish. Take it from me, there ain't no light in the hole. My eyes only shine when the men with the instruments point their shit at me through the bean chute. I'd say they were scientists, but they don't dress like no scientists I've ever seen. Don't talk like them, either.

* * *

I saw what appeared to be a pair of glowing eyes watching me through the food slot. Reports of such phenomena were a common occurrence in 14D.

"Dude!" Todd jerked back from the cell door. "Did you get that?"

Danny whip-panned the camera.

"Get what?"

"I just saw two red fucking eyes in there." He poked his finger towards the slot.

"Are you sure?"

"Yeah, I'm fucking sure. Look at the hair on my arm."

Todd pulled back a sleeve to reveal a toned forearm.

"The night vision doesn't pick it up."

Todd let his arm drop. Danny lowered the camera.

"Dude, did you really see anything?"

Todd's scowl accentuated his widow's peak. He slowly rolled his sleeve back down.

"I thought I did. Do you want to shoot it again?"

Danny shook his head.

"I've gotta change the battery on this thing."

Six-thirty dropped his slop tray and sat next to his fellow GMTs.

When they let you out the hole?

This morning.

You look like shit.

Thank you.

The table laughed. Six-thirty stuck his spoon into the mashed potatoes and it sank to the bottom. He pushed the tray away.

I'll eat it.

A fellow inmate grabbed for the tray. Another inmate, the one who told him he looked like shit, nodded in his direction.

You okay?

Six-thirty just stared at the inmate drinking his potatoes.

You see the man in there? Ol' You-know-who?

Six-thirty looked up, a flash of fear in his eyes, a flash of light.

I am the man.

The table went quiet. The potato drinker slowly lowered his tray.

I awake in the dark of the hole. How did I end up here this time? How long have I been asleep? For all I know, time goes backwards when I'm asleep. There's no way to keep track inside the black.

Some inmates say the beating of your heart is the closest thing to a ticking clock. That's why they call it a ticker. That, and it's like the timer on a bomb, counting down, only you have no idea when it will explode.

I listen past the metronome of my pulse. The Indians are quiet tonight. Maybe they've given up their protest and gone home. Any time I've asked the guards about it they look at me like I'm queer. I know better than to bring it up with my fellow inmates. No tours tonight, either. I'd give anything for some company.

* * *

I'll never forget what happened next. We may have been finished with our investigation, but apparently Alcatraz wasn't finished with us . . .

Todd pulled out the Spirit Box as Danny changed the battery on the camera.

You know we're not rolling," Danny said over his shoulder.

"I know." Todd held the box out in front of him. It issued a blanket of white noise.

"I hate to tell you, but people are gonna get tired of the whole 'it happened off camera' shtick pretty fast."

Todd didn't respond. He just bore imaginary holes into the box's digital display. Danny got to his feet and hoisted his camera bag over his shoulder.

"Come on, man. It's almost morning, and we still gotta shoot the utility corridor." Danny started walking down the hall. "Maybe we'll hear Capone playing his banjo in the shitter."

Todd continued to stare at the display. Halfway down the cellblock, Danny stopped, turned back. Todd had already disappeared from sight.

"You coming, man?" Danny said.

"Man . . ." said the box from the darkness.

What're you in for, anyway?

Six-thirty looked up from the laundry he folded. A man with red skin stood across the table from him. He wore a thick, wool uniform, different from the rest of the inmates.

I'm innocent.

125

The Indian laughed.

It's one thing to say it. But if you want people to believe you're innocent, you have to believe you're innocent.

Six-thirty looked down at his open palms. *The Big Hand and the Little Hand,* his son had called them.

Get back to work! The guard on duty hocked a loogie and spat on the ground. Six-thirty resumed folding.

What're you in here for? Six-thirty asked.

Killed a guard.

What guard?

That one.

The Indian nodded towards the guard behind them. Six-thirty turned to look, but there was no one there. When he turned back around the Indian was gone, too.

I stand in the corner of the hole, watching the man sleeping on the floor. At least I think he's asleep. It's hard to tell, considering I can't really see him. But I can smell him. And as bad as I must smell, he smells worse. I don't know how the guards got him in here without waking me.

I clench and unclench my big hand and my little hand as I think about what to do. The dampness in solitary is murder on the joints. I can yell for the guards, not that they'd come. Or I can wait it out, see if this guy wakes up. Squeaking heralds the arrival of vermin, and I kick to keep them away from the body. I decide to yell.

The bean chute slams open. I look up, only to have a bright light pointed at my face. I turn away, seeing spots, as the guards demand to know who I am and how I got in here.

Send 'im a Chicago Sunset

by Nik Korpon

The needle winked at Capone, a tiny glint of light off the sharp tip.

"Don't fucking look at me like that," he said.

Unfazed, the doctor said, "Keep your arm still," before sticking the needle through Capone's skin and pushing down the plunger, a double dose of penicillin flooding through Capone's flesh. The doctor pressed a cotton ball against the injection spot, pulled out the needle.

"What're y'all playing Sunday? Any new songs?" the doctor said.

"Not sure yet. Working on a thing or two."

The doctor stuck a piece of tape over the cotton ball and said he'd see Capone at the same time tomorrow, then the guard led him away to garden duty.

Capone scrabbled across the ground, the rocks digging into his knees, the dirt stuffed beneath his fingernails. Sweat rolled from his forehead over his temples, soaking into the cotton work shirt's collar. He leaned back on his heels, setting the hand-spade on the ground and paused a moment, the salt-water breeze rolling off the bay cooling his brow. Sometimes, if he listened hard enough, he could hear the nasally honk of cars, the clang and clatter of trolleys, the "L" rattling past one of his warehouses, feel himself in the grandstands at Wrigley, the sun bleeding out red around the building as it disappeared beneath the horizon.

A coolness settled over him. Capone opened his eyes to see a guard backlit against the sun, billy club in hand. "Beauty time's over, 85," he said. "Back to work."

Capone stared at the man long enough to let him know he'd bow to no man—there were more than thirty corpses to back that up—before bending down to pick up the spade and continuing to dig, loosening the soil to make it easier to pull weeds.

The gardens were thick with hollyhock, with snapdragons and bleeding hearts. The only thing the garden needed was a couple cherry trees. He leaned forward, his face deep in the red and blue and purple flowers, and inhaled. His mother, Teresa, would've appreciated a bouquet of these for her kitchen.

The sun was scorching away the shadows when he sunk the spade deep into the earth and felt a sharp click, like he'd hit a large rock or cinderblock buried in the dirt. The ground wasn't the most fertile here, but it wasn't particularly rocky either, especially not in the gardens. He poked the spade around, trying to determine the size of the impediment, but every jab was soft. He pushed the dirt aside with his fingers until he found the hard shape, scraping his index around the outline like excavating a bone, then pulled it out.

It was barely the size of his palm, a crudely carved piece of stone, full of odd edges. Capone brushed away the dirt and held it out in the sun. It vaguely resembled the back of a human figure. The sunlight shifted, slipping behind a bank of clouds, as Capone turned the statue over in his hands. What should've been the face resembled the back of the head, and now what had been the back resembled a face. The more he turned it, the more it shifted, and he began to feel something in his hands—actually, felt something *inside* his hands, like the tremor of joy and fear the first time he fired a pistol, but more electric. Not electric. Powerful.

"85!" the guard barked. His tone said it wasn't the first time he'd called out. Capone slipped the statue inside his sleeve, turned around slowly, and gave the guard a severe look. "Line up for count. Grub's in ten."

Capone could still feel the lingering tremor in his hands, even hours later at dinner. He half-expected to sink his spoon into the bowl of potato chowder and accidentally fling it across the mess hall. Maybe he'd get lucky and it'd land in O'Brien's eyes, blind the guy. That mick had been riding Capone since the day he got transferred to the Rock from Atlanta, giving him looks then pretending he didn't do nothing. If this place wasn't such a stroll compared to the others he'd been in, Capone would've sharpened his fork against the concrete and stuck it in the mick's throat until it came out the other side.

"You gonna eat that zucchini?" Oakes said, sitting across from Capone.

Capone considered the vegetables, then slipped the bowl to the old man when the guard looked away. Oakes was a librarian, came here after robbing a post office in Oklahoma. One of the postmasters had put up a stink; Oakes put two slugs in his face, then a couple in the boy working there

131

just for good measure. He wasn't a bad guy though. Capone liked him well enough.

Capone set the bowl back on his tray once the old man was done. "You know what was here before?"

"We had noodles and meat sauce yesterday," the old man said.

"No, here." Capone jabbed his finger into the table. "This island. Before the big house."

Oakes pushed his wire-rimmed glasses up his nose, rested them on the sharp ridge where the broken cartilage had set unevenly. "Spanish settlers, a hundred-fifty years ago. The Union used it to hold prisoners during the Civil War. Sometimes Indians who didn't want to move off the land."

"Indians, huh?" Capone ladled some chowder onto his spoon, dumped it back into the bowl. When he looked up to ask Oakes another question, he saw O'Brien glaring at him from two tables over.

"The fuck you looking at, you fucking paddy?" Capone said, loud enough that the other men could hear but not so much to throw up flags to the guards.

O'Brien held up his hands, as if saying, *Hey, you got a bone, go blow, pal.*

Capone slammed his fists on the table, went to stand but Oakes laid his hands on Capone's wrists. "Easy, Al. Easy."

Time was, a man would've got lead in the eyes for touching Capone, but Oakes was an okay guy, and anyhow, Capone was tired.

Capone sat on the edge of his bed, banjo resting between his thighs as he tried to perfect a new run he'd been working on. Earlier in the week, he'd struggled with this arrangement, his claw fingers plucking the wrong string, his left-hand fingers tripping as they jumped from note to note. But now, tonight, the music flowed from the banjo, his fingers cascading over frets like a creek over river rock. He caught a glimpse of the statue sitting on the small table beside his bed, which made him pause. His hands thrummed with energy again.

There was a muttering in the cell beside him. Ear cocked, he listened, waiting for O'Brien to repeat himself. When he didn't, Capone spoke up.

"Say it again."

Silence.

"I know what you said, so say it again."

More silence. Across the hall, two inmates whispered to each other.

Capone set the banjo down, walked over to the gate and pressed his face against the metal bars.

"Say 'To hell with you Sicilians,'" he growled. "Say it!"

A loud metallic thwack beside Capone's head made him stumble backward. The guard pulled back his billy club.

"You got a problem, 85?"

"O'Banion thinks he can run his mouth? Thinks I'm some fucking stronzo ain't going to do anything about, does he? Thinks I don't tell everyone in Chicago when to piss and where to do it?" He slammed his hands against the railing but the guard didn't flinch, only gave him a long, considered look.

"Lights out in ten, 85," the guard said. "How about you finish up your practice."

"Lights out," Capone spat. "I'll put his lights out. Make that culo disappear."

The guard looked at him a beat longer before stepping aside.

Capone shoved the banjo away and collapsed on the bed, his body suddenly tired, head filled with smoke. His arm fell to the side, slapping against the table, his fingers grazing the statue. He picked it up without looking, held it in his hands, turning it over and over, examining every edge, every plane, the way the face remained ever-elusive. Like a man disappearing.

Capone glanced at the thick cement wall that separated him and that mick fuck. He set his jaw and squinted his eyes, then gripped the statue tight and focused.

Hastings stepped away from Capone's cell, keeping one eye on the metal bars as if a disembodied arm would suddenly appear and wrap itself around his neck and hurl him over the railing. Warden Johnston had warned Hastings about Capone when he was assigned to this wing, but this? This was something else.

Hastings glanced inside O'Brien's cell, saw the inmate lain back on his bed with a blanket covering his legs and a book propped up in front of his face. A few hunks of dirt—clay maybe, as it looked grey in the evening shadows—speckled the floor at the base of the back wall. It was likely from yard duty, but Hastings had thought O'Brien was on laundry this week.

Hastings rapped his baton against the cell. "90, you giving him lip again?"

O'Brien didn't respond. The book didn't move.

"I'm talking to you."

Hastings felt blood slush through him, felt the heat rising up his neck as he stared at the unmoving inmate. After a long moment, the book shifted a few inches to the side, enough that one eye, eyebrow cocked, was visible.

"Whaddayou think?" he said, his Alabaman drawl making the sentence one long string of conjoined words. "I ain't never even been to Chicago."

The book shifted back. Hastings continued his beat.

A few days later, Hastings was doing the 3:00 a.m. count of his wing. O'Brien lay sideways on his bed, his legs stacked atop each other, arms curled around his head. It looked like there was more dirt on the floor, but it was hard to tell in the dim light. He'd have to tell the inmate to clean his act up if he wanted to keep a cushy position like he had. Hastings went to move on, then paused a moment when he realized he could only see O'Brien's hair, no indication of a face. Just a blackness beneath the arms, like he wasn't really there. Hastings's hand was already going for his keys, his heart pounding at the prospect of an inmate escape, when O'Brien snorted hard and rolled over, his chest heaving like he'd been deprived air.

Hastings took a deep breath and continued the inmate count.

Capone lay in the next cell, hands clasped over his rising chest and thumbs worrying one another in his sleep. The faint light reflected off his eyeballs.

"You're fucking creepy when you sleep with your eyes open, Capone," he said before moving on.

"I ain't sleeping," Capone said to the air. He rubbed his fingers over the statue in his hands, that electric rush from his hands spreading past his arms, up into his shoulders and chest. "I'm waiting."

That Sunday, Capone was standing in line in the mess hall, his fingers tapping out the new banjo run against his thighs.

It was strange, because although he had only practiced it for an hour in the last week, the progression came naturally. He barely had to think, whereas before his playing had stuttered from his intellectualizing the music, trying to plan it. The smell of pounded beefsteak and gravy made his mouth water. He swallowed and turned to the man next to him to comment when he saw O'Brien enter the hall, three men following behind. Their eyes met, and something flashed across O'Brien's eyes before he lowered them to the ground, pausing to let the three men pass by and put more space between him and Capone.

"That's right," Capone said in O'Banion's direction. "That's right." His head went dizzy with the fragrance of roses and tulips mixing with the scent of fresh rain and Hymie Weiss' blood splattered over the wet sidewalk outside Schofield's, O'Banion's flower shop on the North Side of Chicago. He heard the screams of passersby, the faint wail of police sirens, the ting of Tommy-Gun shells hitting concrete.

"That's right," Capone said, turning back toward the meat.

Capone's blood still thrummed through him as he lay in bed that night, the residual effect of a well-played show. The other boys in his band, the Rock Islanders, had picked it up a notch, really giving Capone some decent backing this time to let his banjo shine, like lightning through a cloud, striking squarely on Capone's hands, igniting them, making them move faster than they ever had before. Everything came into sharper focus during the set: the timbre of the inmates' voices yelling *get it, get it* and *play one more*; the smell of dust and sweat and salty air; the trembling of the light on Capone's steel strings as he attacked them. He looked up and over the crowd as they played, and he knew he was almost ready.

Back in his cell, he knew it'd be damn near impossible to sleep, but Capone wasn't planning on sleeping anyhow. Instead, he took the statue in his hands, felt the sensation rush through his body, past his arms, through his chest, shooting through his skull, lighting up new parts of his brain, making his body feel swollen, like a smaller, more powerful being was inflating within his.

He looked over at the wall, felt O'Brien behind it, and blew him a kiss. "How long's it been since you seen a Chicago sunset, pal?"

Capone closed his eyes and focused beyond the wall.

Hastings was still humming a melody as he made his 3:00 a.m. count. He had to give it to the man: that Al Capone could light up a damn banjo. It'd been some years since he'd seen fingers fly like that, not since his uncles' place back in Baltimore. Hastings passed by O'Brien's cell, still adrift on a river of music somewhere in his head, when something in the cell caught his eye. O'Brien was on his side again, in the same exact position as he'd been in the last five nights, his head obscured beneath his arms. Hastings paused at the cell, staring at the blackness where the man's face should be, waiting for him to roll over.

But after two minutes of waiting, the light seemed to shift, and what Hastings had thought was legs looked more like folds in the sheet, propped up with something. What he'd thought were arms, more like twisted pillows. Cold fingers spread through Hastings chest, wove through his ribs, as realization struck.

O'Brien was gone.

* * *

Capone rested his fingers on the statue, no longer able to rub it, as much from the imminent onset of sleep as being physically and mentally exhausted. He couldn't remember ever being this tired before. It was as if all his life force had expanded so frenetically, then collapsed into a single point and drained out the bottoms of his feet. From far away he heard Hastings screaming, "Open the cell! Escaped convict! Escaped convict!"

Capone felt his mouth curl up at the edges as his eyes slipped closed. *That's the thing about a Chicago sunset*, he thought as the statue slipped from his hands.

One minute it's there. And the next?

It ain't.

Creeping

by Gabino Iglesias

"See that *pendejo* leaning against the wall near the water tower?"

Rafa was looking the opposite way, trying to be inconspicuous, Irving nodded. He could see the old man Rafa was referring to. His name was Alvin, but everyone called him "Creepy." Irving worked with him in the kitchen and knew Creepy wasn't a spring chicken, but Creepy moved around the kitchen like nothing hurt and strutted around the yard by himself with an air of confidence Irving had only previously encountered in killers and made men, not small-time thieves or kidnappers. His appearance was unassuming, as well. He had short, spiky hair that he kept combed back, which accentuated his receding hairline. His mouth was a fleshless slit beneath his red, somewhat bulbous nose, and the deep lines around his lips reminded Irving of his *abuelo* Antonio. His mellow eyes under droopy lids reminded Irving of a lazy dog, but he knew this man had a short temper and was always getting into fights. Irving had only been here three weeks, and he had already heard about two separate incidents. Everyone in the kitchen mostly stayed out of Creepy's way.

"So you want me to take him out? Is that it?"

Irving tried to sound annoyed, tried to make it sound as if he was considering doing Rafa a favor and not the other way around. Irving knew his chances of survival were slim if he didn't do what Rafa was asking him to do, but killing Creepy struck him as a steep price to pay for a bit of protection. Irving had killed two men outside before getting caught for kidnapping, so getting his hands bloody wasn't the issue. The problem was there weren't a lot of men in this joint. Just under 300 cats. It'd be hard to shank a guy and disappear into the crowd. Killing a man here sounded like a quick, dumb way to elongate his sentence and earn a stretch in the hole. Still, his options were limited: he had to roll with Rafa and his crew of *boricuas* or try to survive on this damn rock by himself. He had managed fine by himself during the first three weeks, but now things were changing. Rafa insisted on talking to the other Puerto Ricans in Spanish, and a lot of folks disliked that. Racial tension was in crescendo, and not having backup felt like a terrible idea.

Rafa patted Irving on the shoulder, said "You're originally from New York right? You know we Ricans run shit, *mi hermano*. In here, it's no different."

"What's your beef with the old man, Rafa?" Irving asked. He had nothing against making a man bleed for the right reasons, and now any reason would help him feel a little better about this whole deal.

"Creepy has a short fuse, *hermano*. *El tipo* . . . he complains all the time. He gets away with a lot of things. *Es famosillo y eso*. He talks to Bloomquist a lot, sings like a little bird about what goes on when the guards aren't looking. Emérito, Hiram, and I were talking about doing some flying recently. *Dejar el nido. Tú sabes, en español,* but I was translating some of it to keep *mi amigo* Bumpy on the loop. Creepy kept walking by, con *esa cara de comemierda y la sonrisita pendeja esa que siempre tiene en la cara.* I know he heard something. *Debe estar loco por hablar con alguien si no lo ha hecho ya.* Probably wants to wait till he gets something more. No *podemos dejar que eso pase.* You take him out, I owe you, Hiram owes you, and Emérito owes you. We got your back. Boricuas stick together *hasta la muerte.*"

Those words haunted Irving the rest of the day. When you're locked up, being alone is the closest thing to death, and he wanted to feel like he had a crew, someone he could turn to, someone who had his back. Rafa was just a political prisoner, but he was also a man of action, a man not afraid of the authorities. Irving had dealt with many criminals in his life, had learned to read their eyes, and Rafa seemed like he was honest about this. Finally, he made his decision the same way he made all of them: by weighing his fears. In this case, the fear of being alone on The Rock was bigger than the fear of getting caught for shanking the strange, old dude who worked with him in the bakery. The man who swore he was born without fingerprints, though everyone knew they'd been burned off by an underworld quack back in '34.

The kitchen was an open space. The presence of knives meant that the guards kept a close eye on everything the inmates did while prepping the food. Irving knew that getting Creepy in the kitchen was not an option. After they got up, however, and prepared breakfast, the food preppers, cooks, and bakers had a chance to go back and rest for a bit before coming back, or even take a nap if they wanted to eat by themselves instead of joining the rest of the population in the Mess Hall later. That's what Creepy did most mornings, something Creepy had earned after years of service. Creepy's cell was in Block C, closest to The Gas Chamber, as they called the dining hall. Irving's was farther away, in Block A, and fresh meat never got that special treatment. But despite being in different cellblocks, they took the same way out of the kitchen: through the dining hall and then down Broadway before taking different routes.

If Irving timed it right, he could get Creepy in the hallway, right before he turned to return to his cell. That was the only place where he didn't run the chance to being spotted by the guards who stood by the stairs to the Dungeon Cells in front of the library, and at the end of the east corner of the small hallway opposite the Mess Hall, a corridor which ran the length of blocks A, B, and C. Irving knew he could push the man into the first cut-off, which was open and used regularly by guards to access the utility corridor that ran between the two rows of cells. He could stick Creepy and be back in his cell before anyone noticed. He'd have to leave the shiv in Creepy's ribs when he was done sticking and also try to not get any blood on himself, but he hoped the thick layers of clothing and some quick, short stabs would take care of that. There were members of the cleaning crew always up and about, and maybe someone from the laundry room, so even if they saw him following Creepy out of the kitchen, they'd have no evidence to pin the attack on him. If they tried to, he'd just say the old man had jumped him. They would believe it because of Creepy's reputation. As for other inmates, Rafa said he'd make sure everyone kept their mouth shut if they saw anything. Plus, so early in the morning, everyone was still asleep and light was scarce.

Creeping

The day it went down, the kitchen workers were woken up at 4:30 a.m. like always, two hours before the morning whistle. They went to the kitchen and prepared the usual: three large batches of oatmeal, fried bologna sausage, toast, and cottage fried potatoes. Their fellow inmates would wolf it all down exactly two hours and twenty-five minutes later with coffee, milk, and a dab of margarine on their toast, which was made from the bread Creepy baked with his own hands. During Irving's first shift, a guard had told him this breakfast menu had remained the same for two decades, since 1939.

Irving worked quietly, keeping his head down and only occasionally looking around to make sure Creepy wasn't deviating from his morning routine. He skipped the margarine and ate his sausage on top of his toast before lingering over his coffee to wait. Once he finished breakfast, he spent a couple of minutes talking to a guard about the book he was reading and then started making his way out of the kitchen.

By the entrance, a large guard with the unlikely name of Kreaton was scratching a sideburn and looking down at his shoes. He glanced up and opened the gate to let Creepy through. Then while pulling it shut, he saw Irving approaching and swung it wide again.

Irving nodded to the guard and kept walking. Creepy didn't seem to be in a hurry, so catching up to him before the cut-off without having to sprint would not be a problem. He was going to have to make quick work of it though, and try to keep the old man's mouth covered. Suddenly, the echoing of their footsteps was deafening, and he feared everyone was going to wake up and notice the two men walking down the hallway.

145

The cut-off came much sooner than Irving expected. He shoved his hand in his pocket and grabbed the shiv Rafa had given him, a piece of sharpened metal imbedded into a chunk of plastic, wrapped in ribbons torn from an old undershirt for a makeshift grip.

Committed, Irving took two long steps up to Creepy, turned toward him, then brought his left hand up to the old man's mouth and pushed him into the gloominess on the cut-off. But before Irving could stick Creepy, a man appeared next to them, and Irving stopped cold. The figure was taller and thinner than any man he had ever known. Then he noticed it was not a man at all, but more like a shadow. This dark thing raised an arm toward Irving's face, the impossibly long fingers like daggers made from ink. Irving stepped back, and he felt Creepy grab his wrist and twist it hard. He lost his grip on the shiv as Creepy grabbed him by the throat and placed the shiv under his right eye. Irving looked for the black thing, but the number of shadows painting the stone walls were back to normal.

"That was a bad idea, youngster," Creepy said, his breath a foul mix of morning breath, bad hygiene, and coffee. "Baubas always walks with me."

Creepy pocketed the weapon, removed his hand from Irving's throat, and was back out on Broadway with two quick steps. He didn't look back. Irving felt his heart hammering in his throat under Creepy's handprint. He needed to get back to his cell, to sit down and process what had happened. What was he going to tell Rafa? They wouldn't believe a word of it. A tall shadow with impossibly thin hands had kept him from killing Creepy? Those were not facts he was willing to share with anyone. He sucked in air into his lungs and shakily walked out into the hallway.

No one was awake. No faces were pressed against bars. He walked back to his cell replaying the incident in his head, trying hard to convince himself that nerves must have played a trick on him.

Irving knew it almost 10:00 p.m. because the "lights out" count had already happened and the usual whispers and cries were starting to die down. Cell Block A was settling in for the night. He was thinking about his mom, who still lived in Spanish Harlem. One of the worst things about being locked up was not having the opportunity to spend time with her, to give her some money once in a while. Thinking about his mother helped him not to think about what had transpired that morning. He had even claimed he had stomach issues in order to remain in his cell during recess and not have to confront Rafa. He'd have to come up with something else, however, because they wouldn't let him stay inside two days in a row.

Irving sat up on his cot and considered splashing water on his face for focus. He knew sleep was not going to come. The thin, shadow creature was burned into his memory, haunting him. He was rubbing his face when he heard something.

The sound came from the direction of the toilet, a long, loud exhalation. Irving jerked back as he felt icy fingers running down the sides of his torso. He squinted, trying to peel away the darkness and identify the intruder, but to no avail. The sound came again, closer. It reminded him of the last, shaky breath of a dying man. He leaned forward to stand, and something moved in the corner. His heart jumped, and he scooted back on his cot until he ran out of space.

Something darker than the shadows was growing behind the toilet, climbing the walls and emerging slowly from the gloom. It was the tall, thin shape that had saved Creepy in the cut-off. Mind reeling, Irving jumped off his cot and pressed his back against the bars of his cell. The thing moved toward him, gliding through the air with ease and emitting the same exhaling sound once more.

In the next second, Irving finally understood why a man like Alvin was still living despite picking so many fights. He also realized why he'd been the only of his crew captured alive. Lastly, he recognized that this old man they called Creepy would exist for years to come, but that his own expiration date had been rolled forward by something he couldn't begin to comprehend.

At the end, Irving did the one thing he had promised himself he'd never do while in prison: he screamed. And the sound started as an agonizing, primal plea, but soon flattened into something between a wet cough and a whimper as the shadow's long fingers disappeared into fluttering muscles of Irving's throat.

Two cell blocks down, Alvin "Creepy" Karpis looked up at the ceiling, the smile that had earned him his peculiar nickname plastered on his face. As the last echoes of the scream died, the man with no fingerprints closed his eyes and sent out the only prayer his mom had taught him that he still remembered: "Thank you, Baubas. Thank you now and always."

Stash

by Dino Parenti

San Francisco, CA, 5/28/70

The bus squealed to a halt at Townsend and the Embarcadero, and two boys in olive canvas jackets and bloated backpacks doddered out. A forever dapple of gull guano cued them into checking the bottoms of their Keds, their efforts languid as legs had turned Gumby on them around Gilroy.

"Damn, it's chilly," said Sean, with his wide-eyed gawk and ledged lower lip, hugging elbows in a vein effort to stopper gales lancing every stitch of clothes. At fourteen, he'd yet to venture past Bakersfield to the north and Disneyland to the south, rubber-stamping in advance his tourist rank in the eyes of locals.

No sooner had he lit a cigarette, Corey lip-farted at the remark, despite the chill plundering his virgin bones, too. Though also fourteen, he'd doubled his friend's scope, having sampled the soil from San Jose to Ensenada, respectfully. But Bay Area cold ran hostile over soft hides, a warning Corey dismissed with dramatic eye rolls and smirks that could cut stone. He declared that no trespass was worth undertaking without some element of risk and discomfort, especially if it discomforted the local fuzz.

Sean pointed at the squat warehouse atop piles. "There's Pier 40! And I bet that's *The Clearwater!*"

Corey grimaced. "A little louder, butthole. I don't think they heard you in Sausalito." And he blew a streamer of smoke to conceal a shiver.

"Sorry," Sean muttered. He slid hands down his jacket, personally magic-markered with peace signs, anti-war slogans, and song lyrics by The Birds and The Doors, an emulation of any number of returning vets he'd seen on TV. He checked his watch. "Boat leaves in ten."

Corey pitched his half-smoked butt. "Let us *endeavor* then."

TRANSCRIPT EXCERPTS

Recorded at Holy Light Retirement Home, Miami, FL, 6/2/16, 2:00 p.m., EST.

INTERVIEWER: Sean Able Paredes (SAP), 59, owner of website, The ApolloInitiative.com.

SUBJECT: Meryl Leonard Fross (MLF), 91, former Alcatraz inmate.

Time stamp: (4:32 of 19:51)

MLF: Remind me again why we're talking?

SAP: Oh, as the email said, I'm writing a book. On the 1962 escape?

MLF: A book, huh?

SAP: Mr. Fross, you approached me, remember?

MLF: Yes! So I did. Sorry. Noodle ain't what it used to be.

SAP: Whose is? Do you remember the dates you served?

MLF: Just 4 months in '62, for armed robbery. Before transfer to McNeil Island.

SAP: And in that period, you gained intimate knowledge of the escapes of Frank Morris and John and Clarence Anglin?

MLF: Oh, indeed I did.

SAP: Okay then. Let's begin.

Getting aboard *The Clearwater* wasn't hard. Not for Corey.

He approached the two men loading boxes of Campbell's Soup and drinking water, and asked for passage to Alcatraz, claiming to be Hopi from Arizona.

The two men—genuine Indians—sized up the boys. Swapped dubious glances that wilted once Corey tossed them each a fresh pack of Salem's, and they were off.

Passing under the Bay Bridge an hour later, the ornery chop nudging the repurposed trawler perpetually west, they at last spotted the mound of Alcatraz in the distance sifting through an inbound veil of fog. Campfires pinpricked the southern headlands, the government having cut off the power and water that very morning.

"Did you know a Geronimo contemporary did time there after the Civil War?" asked Sean. "That as many prisoners were native peoples as were gangsters?"

Corey tried to pass off his seasickness as ants-in-the-pants discomfort. "That a fact?"

"A stone-cold one."

They said nothing more on route, having exhausted their words on the bus ride from L.A. In hushed, excited bursts, they spoke of the famed stash of contraband supposedly accrued by the four wardens of Alcatraz, hidden away in the mansion by the lighthouse. And while Sean also looked forward to mingling with the Indians who'd staked out the island for over a year, claiming it as tribal land, Corey's lure hinged on the possibilities of booze, grass, and girls. He consigned the famed 1962 escape and Indian affairs to tourists. Yet he was willing to share in the grounding risk with Sean, what with both their parents collectively new-aging under the presumption their boys were headed to 4-H camp in Big Sur.

That lie alone sold him on the exploit.

Time stamp: (7:08 of 19:51)

SAP: Wait. Earlier you said you only spoke to Allen West in the yard. Now you claim he was your cell neighbor?

MLF: Yuh-huh. His cell was B-140. Mine was B-142.

SAP: And West told you escape details?

MLF: In a roundabout way. The man was a terminal mutterer. Happened a lot inside. The isolation and all. I guess he figured he was being quiet, but at night you could hear fleas fucking in the basement. He kept repeating the plan: raft to Angel Island, then swim the Raccoon Strait to Tiburon, then steal a car and drive north. Sometimes he'd even mention a boat to San Diego, and contacts in Mexico. Man, Morris kept shushing him day and night. He was West's neighbor opposite. Cell B-138.

SAP: Did you know Frank Morris?

MLF: Naw. Seen him in the mess, of course, but he carried a bad air with him. Like if he'd caught you staring, he'd have chewed out your eyes.

SAP: Never heard that one.

MLF: So you really spent time on The Rock with them Indian squatters, huh?

SAP: About 9 months, yes.

MLF: That a fact?

SAP: (laughter) A stone-cold one.

MLF: Man, if I had a buck for every swarthy some-bitch claimed he camped with them Alcatraz Indians, I could've bought The Rock myself by now.

SAP: You don't believe me?

MLF: Look, Poncho, everyone needs their stories. Their myths. Lies and self-delusion keep the clocks wound.

SAP: What if I told you I slept on the warden's bed, too?

MLF: Really? You know, from my cell, I could see the top of that damn house from the gallery windows? Always daydreamed of dropping a monster shit on Warden Johnston's pillow. Too bad your people burnt the place down.

SAP: Well, accidents happen.

MLF: That what it was? 'Cause my understanding, official report was inconclusive.

SAP: As you've said, people need their stories. Let's get back to West and Morris . . .

Three days of tent speeches, fire-dances, and waving at the ubiquitous Coast Guard cutter circling the island, and a state-of-the-union meeting for all 324 inhabitants of Alcatraz was finally called by the acting leader of The Indians of All Tribes in the recreation yard.

Sean waited by the north service entrance of the warden's house when Corey finally appeared.

"Is that blood?" Sean asked of the smears on Corey's arms and forehead that the cutter's sweeping lights inflamed in quick bursts.

Corey glanced at his skin, and shrugged. "Nope. Just helped this crazy Navaho paint some graffiti on the water tower though."

"Well, we probably *had* an hour, tops," said Sean. Corey had been toking steady from the moment they'd docked, and Sean wondered if his friend even realized the terra cotta shade of the paint he used matched that of the Golden Gate Bridge. "You sure you're ready for this?"

Corey noogied a knuckle into Sean's chest.

"Hell yeah I'm ready! As in an I-just-met-this-cool-beatnik-chick-from-Oregon-who's-aching-for-some-liquor ready, you catch my drift, son?"

Sean nodded despite the guilt riming his veins. Not the safe, lilywhite guilt of anticipation on the ride over, but the ice-hard shame of actual violation in progress. He'd come to sympathize with the American Indian Movement and their mission. Between his explorations of the cellblocks for escape clues, he'd befriended some of the leadership and inquired of their personal stories, but when asked to reciprocate, he'd found himself twisting his half-Mexican, yet privileged, heritage into a yarn of subjugated Aztec plight.

"Now to get in . . ." he said.

Corey winked, then dropped suddenly to all fours with a dramatic flourish and crawled to an array of potted petunias by the door and lifted the only spray of purple amongst pink. A brass key winked underneath, and he grinned up at Sean, eyes glinting naughty. "It's a prison, son. Cigarettes equal gold. Now let's find us some booty."

Time stamp: (12:13 of 19:51)

MLF: I'm telling you, Poncho, they drowned! Ain't no

way they survived those currents and that cold. Not the Anglins, not Morris with his goddamned genius IQ. Didn't you see the movie? Even Eastwood couldn't have swum that shit.

SAP: I've studied Alcatraz my whole life, Meryl. I know all the tales. Give me something not from Wikipedia.

MLF: Okay. West blubbered all night in his cell after he couldn't break through the roof, whining how he also screwed up busting out of a Florida pen the year before. He admitted to guard help there, so research that. Runty-looking bastard. Always stunk of moleskin. When the guards dragged him out in the morning, his things were still tied around his ankle.

SAP: Interesting.

MLF: Still don't believe me, huh?

SAP: Frankly, I question if you even did time on the Rock.

MLF: Yeah? Well screw off then.

SAP: Between 1,557 and 1,576 prisoners served in Alcatraz, depending on the lists. That's a 19-prisoner disparity. Maybe you were too transitional. Possible they kept poor records for turnarounds under 6 months.

MLF: I personally know of ten men who did short time there before transfers. I'll give you names. If you can't find at least one, feel free to call me a liar.

SAP: Convenient, since they're likely all dead by now.

MLF: Know what? I don't believe you either.

SAP: Believe what?

MLF: Your bullshit. That you were ever there. With the Indians. Living in the warden's mansion before it burned.

SAP: Except I know exactly how that happened.

MLF: Yeah? Injun reprisal? Getting back at whitey?

SAP: You really want to know?

MLF: What's the catch?

SAP: Your full confession that you're not Meryl Fross, but are in fact, Frank Morris.

The boys borrowed the full moon and slicing shafts of light the Coast Guard provided to move about the mansion.

Corey whistled upon entering the foyer. Marveled at all the oak paneling and detailing the plain exterior belied.

"Fancy-schmancy," he said. "Wayne Manor had a baby."

"Did you know Al Capone tried to bribe Warden Johnston into letting him sleep in one of the mansion bedrooms instead of his cell?" Sean asked.

"That a fact?"

"A stone-cold one."

Corey simpered at Sean's sluggish gaping of the space. Of *everything* since their arrival, really. He'd long worried of his friend's faraway gazes. Of eyes that pushed at outlying barriers, and of a brain that perpetually approached escape velocity, threatening to leave the world behind.

"Paper, rock, scissors," Corey announced suddenly.

"For what?"

"Just play along, huh, butt-wipe?"

They shook fists three times, and Sean's scissors caved under Corey's rock, and Corey said, "You get the downstairs, I got the upstairs. Holler if you find anything."

Corey took the stairs two at a time, just as the Coast Guard cutter brayed its hourly bullhorn call for their peaceful retreat from Alcatraz.

Sean explored the living and dining rooms. Studied all the paintings and photographs on the walls. He poked his head into the maid's quarters, then into a game room of pressed-tin ceiling tiles and a billiard's table the size of a Cadillac Fleetwood, and eventually he wandered into the parlor.

Behind a walnut desk, several glass cases had been inset within the bookshelves, and when he peered in he couldn't believe his eyes.

Four papier-mâché masks of crude half-faces resting on velvet pillows.

From what he'd read, he knew the hair was real, smuggled from the prison barbershop. The "flesh," a composite of water, toilet paper, and sawdust from the woodshop. And as the cutter's lights swept through the windows, he beheld a rapid snapshot of each decoy of the men who'd broken out, glimpsing them how he imagined the passing guards did at night, and he realized that for split-second looks, the masks passed muster. Just as he was about to call out to Corey, the other's voice yelled from upstairs for him to come up.

Sean ascended the stairs, and at the top landing made out a sliver of flickering yellow at the end of the nearly pitch-black hall. He pushed open the door and entered the southernmost room, likely the warden's master suite. A large four-poster bed and fireplace. A pair of tall windows framing a dolled-up San Francisco across the Bay.

"Corey?"

"In here," came the muffled reply from a side door.

Sean peered in. Old clothes draped in butcher paper hung from rods along both walls. At the rear, they'd been shifted aside to reveal a secondary door, low and narrow.

"Corey, you won't believe what I found downstairs!"

A moment later, Corey emerged cradling a box overflowing with *Playboy* magazines and bottles of whiskey.

"Glad now I brought so many cigarettes?" he replied, smirking.

"Holy crap . . ."

Corey nodded. "Eureka, son."

Time stamp: (14:04 of 19:51)

MLF: See, that's bullshit, too. Morris hailed from DC. I'm Baltimore, born-and-bred.

SAP: Ex-cons are creatures of habit. They think they're clever, even after caught lying red-handed.

MLF: Ha! Shows what you know.

SAP: How'd you survive that swim? How'd you avoid the dragnet afterwards?

MLF: Mine ain't to prove. You're the DA, Poncho.

SAP: Your flips are showing, Frank.

MLF: How'd that mansion really burn? (Sounds of paper rustling)

SAP: Your last registered license plate in 1997 was Georgia, 1441ZA. AZ1441 was Frank Morris's prisoner number. You asked specifically for this room for the view. Room 831. The reverse of Frank's cell in Alcatraz, 138. You claim birth directly across a river. Hell, even your initials are reversed. Meryl Leonard Fross. Frank Lee Morris.

(Clicking sound)

MLF: What's the piece for, Poncho?

SAP: For the truth. I got you, jailbird. And my name's not Poncho. And it's not Sean either.

(Muffled pop)

Under candlelight, they explored file-box after file-box, rifling the contents and wowing at the plethora of improvised shivs while chortling at *Archie* comics and stacks of *Life Magazine* defaced by the more creative and vulgar inmates. Mustaches on women. Peckers for men's noses.

Corey arrayed confiscated booze by proof level. Piled *Playboys* by year, and after a while, by month as another box overflowing with buxom covers was fleshed out. Sean marveled at his friend's seemingly conjured-from-the-ether sense of organization. Suddenly he'd merged a museum curator to a horny tomcat. At one point, Corey dragged a box from the lowest shelf, opened it, and foot-shoved it to the side to join the "boring" pile, and only because he'd replaced the lid with a date printed on one corner did Sean notice it.

"Holy hell, Corey!" he yelped, yanking off the lid.

"What? Hey, have you seen a Bettie Page issue? Should be January 1955. I'd screw a chicken for a spread of that woman."

Sean pointed at the box and at last said, "6/12/62? That's the date. The date they escaped."

"Who?"

"*Who?* Frank Morris? The Anglin Brothers?"

Corey's mouth-O suggested a crowning egg in the offing before cracking to a raspberry. "Well there you go. Say, why don't you take that into the other room and solve the great mystery, huh? I'll handle the boobs."

But Sean was already halfway out with the box. He upended the contents on the merlot satin bedspread, puffing combers of dust in all directions.

Dossiers on the three escapees made up the heaviest items, plus a couple that had aided and abetted, including Allen West, the fourth con who couldn't cut his way to the roof in time. The remaining material consisted of handwritten notes on prison stationary, mugshots, guard interviews, and assorted schedules dating back a month before the escape.

So absorbed he'd become perusing the ephemera that he almost didn't notice Corey heal-toeing to the bathroom.

"What's up?" Sean asked.

Corey froze. In his hands, a candle like the one in the closet, with a stack of *Playboys* tucked under his arm.

"Nature calls," he said, smiling sheepish, and shuffled quickly into the bathroom.

The squeal of a draw bolt. Sean shrugged and resumed his study.

The final item he cleared space for at the foot of the bed and accordioned open. A nautical survey of the Bay. Alcatraz and Angel Island. X's scribed in red marker on the southwest shore of Angel, with three dotted lines leaving Alcatraz. From there, two dotted lines running north to Sausalito, with a third shooting west, under the Golden Gate Bridge and off the map altogether.

For each set of lines, a set of three numbers ending in question marks, and his pulse double-timed. He'd seen enough *McHale's Navy* and *Sea Hunt* to recognize coordinates anywhere.

Had the escapees survived after all? Did these bearings reveal their destinations?

So oblivious to time he'd become that at first he attributed the smell of smoke to his imagination going full-tilt. But then a flushed, coughing Corey stumbled out of the bathroom a moment later, a full grey billow trailing him.

"We gotta scram," he said, and stiff-walked towards the door, buckling his pants.

The bathroom suddenly flared yellow and hot. Flames licked up the drapes, catching from the charring, wilting magazine opened at what Sean guessed was a Linda Gamble centerfold, carefully perched atop a soap dish opposite the toilet.

His friend's hangdog face hovered by the door. "I . . . tried to put it out," he said, before turning defensive at Sean's glare. "I accidentally kicked over the candle as I . . . Never mind! Leave that crap and let's go!"

Outside, and already the fire had blown out the bathroom window and a wooly, leaden column rose against the moon. Men were running from the rec yard, yelling for hoses and buckets. The boys ducked behind a garden wall and waited for a more substantial crowd to get lost in, but by then the whole mansion was engulfed, casting its secrets to the sky in flame and embers.

Time stamp: (16:48 of 19:51)

MLF: That's a quality silencer, but you don't aim too good, son. Pull 6 inches to your right next time.

SAP: I wasn't trying to kill you, Frank. Just expose you. It's what I do.

MLF: Then you do what you gotta, and I'll do what I gotta. Let the world outrun us both.

SAP: Not a chance. Goodbye, Frank. Gotta catch a flight.

END OF INTERVIEW
PROPERTY OF MIAMI DADE COUNTY POLICE

Disembarking *The Clearwater* at Pier 40 the morning after fire gutted the warden's house to its concrete bones, as several plain-clothed cops greeted the first of the exodus.

They searched and questioned the passengers, and when

they patted down Corey, they found a folded *Batman* comic stuffed in his back.

Had he kept his mouth shut instead of griping about unreasonable search-and-seizure, he might've been allowed to keep it. But they flipped through it, likely looking for smuggled weed, and a dozen *Playboy* centerfolds spilled onto the dock instead, catching in the wind and flashing skin at everyone. The cops scowled at Corey, gathered up the "evidence," and only chortled after sending him off.

Sean offered no resistance to their pat-downs and questions, and they only harrumphed at the peacenik doodles on his jacket. Scribbles supplemented with a series of three, tri-number sets on his sleeves and lapels. Numbers likely mistaken for dates or Bible verses, for anything besides a future plan, and Sean grinned wide the whole bus-ride home.

Miami, FL, 6/4/16

Forty-eight hours after the crackpot interviewer left, Meryl saw him again, albeit on television.

The nurse changing his bedpan scowled ugly when the anchor reported a naked man had streaked the stage during a TED Talk in New Orleans the previous evening.

"A discussion of parallel universes and chaos theory turned downright prophetic Friday night when 59 year-old Sean Paredes, of Los Angeles, jumped the stage, and upon taking the microphone from the speaker, commenced on a conspiracy theory tirade before security wrestled him to the floor. Closed-circuit television captured the event . . ."

Meryl peered at the screen over the thickset nurse wiping him down. Watched the same man who put a slug in his pillow not two days earlier bumble bare-assed towards the mousy guy talking on stage, nethers pixilated. He grabbed the mic and screamed into it:

"You're being lied to, people! Behold, a descendent of Apollo before you! God of knowledge and intellect! Because I know! I know Jimmy Hoffa's in witness protection in Montana! D.B. Cooper's a Wall Street broker, still stealing! And Frank Morris is alive and well in Miami! Because people leave clues! They always leave clues!"

Two security guards tackled him then, though he managed to yell an *"Apollo-Initiative-dot-com!"* before being hauled offstage.

Meryl ground his dentures. Gripped the .38 hidden under his blanket.

"That poor soul," said the nurse.

"He's right, you know?" said Meryl. "That's me."

The nurse sighed. "Who, hon?"

"Frank Morris. Escaped Alcatraz, June 12, 1962."

The nurse patted his hand. "I'll send in Dr. Willamette, hon. He'll start you back on Haldol. Remember, Jesus loves you."

"That's a fact," he muttered as she walked out. "A stone-cold one. Jesus loves all his daredevils."

Roller Canary
By Max Booth III

The key was to keep the ends closed. Castle your king as soon as possible. Protect your main man no matter the consequences. The guard, McKenzie, either didn't understand this philosophy or didn't give a shit. The young chap was too eager, too full of cum and adrenaline to collaborate his thoughts into a decent strategy. He charged onward in a direct, predictable path, a soldier on the frontline who'd learned how to reload his firearm the previous morning.

"You ought to take your time," Stroud said. "We're in no rush here."

McKenzie chuckled despite the vermillion burning in his cheeks. "Maybe you ain't in no rush. Me? I got a wife and kid to go home to this afternoon. Hot, home-cooked meal on the table waiting for me."

"How sweet."

"Fuck you, Birdman. You wish you had my life—hell, *any* life. You? After this, you'll just go back to a bunk and play with your little sore-infested pecker. Rinse and repeat until old age eventually rots you out. It's your turn, by the way."

Stroud stared at the board. Another four moves and the Leavenworth guard's fate would be secured. Three if he was even dumber than Stroud anticipated.

"You know, I'm not as alone and miserable as you so gleefully wish to believe." Stroud made his move, waited for the guard to figure out his inevitable defeat. "Incarceration does not mandate solitude."

"Are you talking about your fuckin' birds again?"

"Companionship is not restricted to humanity."

"You can't be friends with birds. That's just not right." McKenzie paused, thumb softly caressing the head of a bishop. "Wait. You don't . . . touch them, do you?" He leaned over the board, genuine concern in his eyes. "Please tell me you don't fuck those birds."

Stroud smirked and nodded at the board. "I'd think wisely about that next move, if I were you."

The guard settled back in his seat, mortified. The truth was, Stroud had never touched the birds inappropriately, but he did enjoy entertaining the rampant rumors of his strange predilections, as well as screwing with the guards and his fellow inmates every chance he got. He truly loved his birds with a great passion. Loved them like family. The birds permitted him a purpose to breathe. Without them in his life he doubted he would have survived the last twenty years.

McKenzie simulated deep concentration. "You know, to be honest, I still don't quite understand why we even let you keep them. Tell me how a violent murderer gets to have pets. Tell me how that makes sense."

Now it was Stroud's turn to lean over the board, a grim grin upon his lips. "Have any guards fallen at my hand since my adoption of ornithology?"

Stroud resisted the urge to remind McKenzie that he'd been a resident of this penitentiary more years than the guard had been alive. That at this point he knew more about the job than McKenzie would ever know. The simple truth was the prison granted him permission to keep his birds because it kept him busy, productive. A smart prison focused on activity rather than punishment. A smart prison actually gave a shit about its inmates.

It was very clear McKenzie did not belong here. And if Stroud didn't fear a prohibition on his birds, he'd attend to the matter himself.

Finally McKenzie said, "What the fuck is *ornithology?*"

And Stroud laughed, loud and true. Then he moved his queen down the board. "Checkmate."

"Oh, you son of a bitch."

The guard looked over Stroud's shoulder and tapped his watch, then nodded. Stroud followed his stare and caught another guard standing at the prison yard entrance moments before he disappeared. Stroud didn't miss a beat.

"We got time for another game." The guard nodded at the chessboard. "Interested?"

"I think I'd rather just return to my cell, if it's all the same to you."

He attempted to rise, but the guard grabbed his wrists and held them against the table. "Actually, it's not all the same to me."

"No?"

McKenzie nodded at the board. "Sit. Play. Enjoy yourself."

If he resisted any further, the guard would not hesitate to issue violence. You serve long enough and you learn the rules of the pen. When a guard had a look in his eyes like

McKenzie did, you obeyed whatever he ordered, unless you wanted a broken nose, unless you wanted another life sentence thrown at you.

Stroud smiled again, this time artificial and strained. "Okay. Let's play."

In another week Bobby Stroud would be nineteen years old, and he had shit to show for it. He'd run away at age thirteen and since then had only visited his family once, nearly two years ago now. His drunk of a father he could go the rest of his life without talking to again, and the sooner cirrhosis ate up his liver, the better. But he missed his mother and siblings dearly.

Like they really needed him. They seemed to be doing a whole lot better without him in their lives now that they had money. Not a lot, but they weren't as poor as they'd been when he was a kid. One less mouth to feed. One less burden. Maybe it was better it stayed that way. Standing out in the cold, holding a package of salmon he'd bought off a street vendor, he wondered if he'd ever get around to visiting them again. Alaska was a big territory, connected to an even bigger country, and there was still much of it left to explore.

Although, at this point, he was pretty goddamn sick of Juneau. He should have never talked Kitty into moving here with him. The place was a shithole if he'd ever seen one. But so was everywhere, when you really thought about it.

It was that Russian fucker Charlie's fault. Kitty's old friend or ex-lover—he wasn't sure which. Probably didn't want to know the truth anyway. In fairness, Bobby realized he had no room to criticize whom she'd slept with. You couldn't pimp out your girlfriend then give her shit about who's been inside her. The world didn't rotate that way. But there was something about this Charlie asshole that didn't quite sit right with him. Maybe it was the way he dressed, like he was better than everybody else. Or the way he exaggerated and bragged about things that didn't count for nothing, when in reality he was just as full of shit as anybody, if not more so.

Sure, back in Cordova, it had been a different story. The way Charlie spoke about Juneau made it sound like a magical land of promise and prosperity. In retrospect, maybe Charlie had only been trying to steal Kitty from him. It made sense. What Kitty lacked with youth, she more than made up for with beauty. Any young man would kill for a piece of her. And if not kill, they'd at least pay good money, as Bobby had soon discovered. Kitty didn't seem too upset about it. In fact, it'd been her idea to start up again in the first place. Back in Katalla, where they first met, she'd been making a healthy living as a whore. It made sense, at least until Bobby could find a new job in Juneau. Six months they'd been in this fucking place, and success seemed unreachable. At least in Cordova people would hire him. He'd made an impressive amount of cash on the railroads there. It was hard, exhausting work, but the pay was worth it. Only a fool would have quit such a job.

Bobby Stroud laughed in the middle of the street, feet buried in snow. It amazed him, sometimes, the paths people took. One day you're a thirteen-year-old kid getting whipped by your drunk father, the next you're nineteen with a prostitute for a girlfriend, unemployed, and just as hopeless as ever. What awaited his life one year from now? Would he even still be in Alaska? Would he still be with Kitty? The uncertainty of it all fueled him onward. Some people feared mystery. Bobby thrived on it.

An owl's hoot echoed in the night, and Bobby spotted a

small boreal perched atop a cottage, staring straight at him. Hesitant, he raised his hand and waved. For a moment he was convinced it would wave back at him, but a woman's scream shattered their shared silence and scared the owl away.

Up ahead, the screaming woman stumbled toward him. The blood did a wonder of disguising her identity, but it took no time at all for him to recognize Kitty. Bobby dropped the packaged salmon and bolted forward, catching her just as her legs surrendered to gravity. He carried her off the street and laid her gently into the snow. There was no question what had happened. Clearly a john had gotten too rough. It'd happened in the past, but never this bad.

"Where is he?" Bobby already envisioned his fists breaking the man's face. He wouldn't kill him, but he'd make him wish he was dead.

Kitty spat something thick and hard out of her mouth. "Charlie . . ."

"What?" Bobby pulled her up, forced her eyes to meet his. "What did you say?"

"He's crazy . . . Charlie . . . he . . . I'm so sorry . . ."

"It's okay." He hugged her tight, rage pumping and keeping him warm. "It's okay."

"You know, I've never been given a straight answer," McKenzie said, falling into Stroud's trap and replacing one of his pawns with a rook.

"To what are you referring?"

"The birds."

Stroud sighed. "Do you honestly believe I would fornicate with—"

McKenzie held up his hand. "No, obviously you don't

fuck birds, man. I'd have know about that. What I mean is, *why* birds? How did it start? Why do you even *give* a shit?"

Stroud considered his answer. He could have told him the long story. How he found the injured canaries twenty-some years ago in the prison yard, just when the dark thoughts started to become truly unbearable. How he raised them back to perfect health and set them free. He could have told him how birds listened better than any human being he'd ever met. How he'd never felt more at home than in his cell with his books and birdcages. How the universes had aligned to implant Robert in this spot, that his destiny was right here, advancing ornithology into the second half of the twentieth century. Birds were his purpose. It took many years to learn this truth, but now that he understood, he would dedicate the rest of his life to the cause.

Stroud cleared his throat, stared seriously at the guard. "What is the one thing these birds have that every inmate here desires?"

McKenzie shrugged.

Stroud pointed up. "Flight."

"You want to fly, old man?"

"Could you imagine the possibilities?"

The guard chuckled and moved his queen. "Where would you fly?"

"Maybe back to Alaska."

Only he'd fly back in time, too, redo it all. Embrace ornithology earlier in life. Life is so short, and knowledge so infinite. If he'd started his research in his teen years; maybe he would have actually been able to accomplish something worthwhile.

"What makes you think anybody still cares about you there?" the guard asked.

"Oh, believe me. They don't."

"No?"

"I miss the snow."

"It snows here."

"It doesn't snow here."

Stroud slid his bishop down the board. "Well, no place snows like Alaska more than Alaska. Checkmate."

McKenzie checked his watch and sighed. "One more game?"

He found the Russian in his cottage, a ball of snow pressed against his bruised knuckles. At the sight of Bobby, Charlie jumped up from the dining room table and backed against the wall.

"Now, just hear me out, all right? It's not what you think."

It didn't matter what Charlie had to say. Words were useless at this point. Bobby struck him once, twice, then threw him across the table. Waited for him to get up, then kicked him in the face.

Maybe Bobby's misfortunes couldn't be blamed on the Russian. Not all of them. Not most of them. But goddammit it felt good to finally have a visage that differed from his own reflection to direct the guilt. Three more punches and Charlie stopped moving, but the rage hadn't come close to dying down. He hit him a few more times, then pulled out the pistol from the back of his trousers and pressed it against the Russian's head.

"Speak," he said, but received no response.

He pulled the trigger.

After he cleaned off his face, he wrestled Charlie's wallet from his pocket and headed out the door. Before his rampage, he'd recruited the aid of a neighbor to assist with

Kitty's wellbeing. Now, halfway to the neighbor's cottage, an unknown force halted him in his tracks.

Where do you go from here? a silent voice cried, alien and raw.

He looked at the wallet in his swollen hand and dropped it in the snow. It disappeared. Somewhere, a boreal whispered secrets, and Bobby listened and understood with perfect clarity. He couldn't go back. Not now. Not to Kitty, not to his family down in Washington. Some things couldn't be reversed. Some things couldn't be erased from existence no matter how hard you blinked.

He gave the neighbor's cottage a farewell glance and turned around.

Oh, Kitty. I'm sorry.

It was a fifteen-minute walk to the police station.

"Aren't you married?" Smugness ran freely across the guard's face, asking questions he already knew the answers to.

"I'd rather not discuss my marriage." Robert Stroud lowered his head, tried to focus on the game.

"It's been a few years since you've been allowed to see her, ain't that right?"

Stroud grunted and thought, *More like five years,* but stayed silent. He looked at the board, but all he saw were the faces of the women in his life. His mother, who'd disowned him at the discovery of his secret marriage. Della, his wife and partner in ornithology, permanently banned from visiting him. And Kitty. Sweet, beautiful Kitty, her namesake the natural enemy of birds everywhere.

He had let all of them down.

The guard cracked his knuckles. "But you never really gave a shit about her, did you?"

This got Stroud's attention. "Excuse me?"

McKenzie shrugged. "Just, you know, rumor is, she was just some cock-hungry prison fanatic who wrote letters to you about birds. Then you manipulated her into marriage as a way to avoid transfer to the Rock."

"Look up at the sun," Stroud said, not taking the bait. "You can describe it as bright, but surely you understand it isn't that simple."

"Uh-huh." McKenzie laughed. "Whatever the fuck that means." He focused on the game for a moment, captured Stroud's rook. "Do you miss her?"

"I miss everything," Stroud said, softly, vulnerable, and he was reminded of the Eurasian crow which shared the name of his fallen chess piece.

"You think you're gonna write another book?"

"Have you read my other work?" Stroud raised his brow, doubtful.

The guard snorted. "I'm not really the reading type."

"A very surprising statement."

"Prick."

"I trust you've heard about Roller Canary."

McKenzie stared at him blankly.

"The publisher of *Diseases of Canaries*. My book."

Recognition clicked. "Oh, yeah. They ripped you off, right?"

Stroud nodded. "In my age, I've come to learn penitentiary walls do nothing to separate the criminals. They inhabit this world both inside and out."

"What, he didn't pay you royalties, so you bitched about him in some magazine, and now he's trying to get you transferred?"

"That's what I hear."

"You think he'll be successful?"

"I think you already know the answer to that."

"You could have just let it go. So what if he didn't pay. Not like you can spend shit, anyway, Hemingway."

"It was going to my mother." Stroud groaned, holding his side. His body suddenly ached. "Another thing I've come to learn the hard way."

"What's that?"

"That it's not a crime to victimize a person behind bars. Once the jumpsuits get thrown on, inmates cease their occupation as human beings and devolve into government property. You can do whatever you want to them."

The smile on the guard's face appeared almost reptilian. "And what's wrong with that? You ain't exactly innocent, old man."

"Show me someone who is." Stroud maneuvered his knight into an "L," considered announcing checkmate, but couldn't find the energy.

"You know," the guard said, moving a pawn down the board, not yet realizing he'd already lost, "you're a lot of things, but you ain't stupid."

"I don't know what I am."

"You know what's going on here." He motioned to the empty prison yard. It was just the two of them—had been for some time now. "You know what's happening."

"I believe I have an idea."

"Yeah?"

Stroud nodded, eyes difficult to keep open. He'd been exhausted his entire life, and it only worsened with age. "Leavenworth finally received its approval."

When McKenzie nodded, there was genuine empathy in his eyes. "It took some time. Hell, years, really. I guess it's been in the process since before I started here. You can thank your publisher for helping speed things up!"

"One could claim writers have less rights than prisoners."

"Are you going to put up a fight?"

Stroud coughed out a laugh. "What could this body do? My bones are the equivalent of a rotten log covered in moss. One touch and I'll crack."

"You gonna send out more of your petitions?"

"Will I be given the opportunity?"

"I doubt it. Not where you're going."

"Alcatraz."

Stroud settled back in his chair, weak and surrendered. The word sounded foreign coming from his lips. He could visualize the color draining from his sickly flesh. He thought of roller canaries, birds routinely sacrificed by miners, suffocating underground in their cages after singing through closed beaks all their lives.

"What will—" He choked on phlegm and cleared his throat, focused his deteriorating vision on the guard. What he spoke again, it came out as a weak whisper. "What will be done with my birds?"

"Already done removed from your cell."

"Where—where will they go?"

The guard shrugged. "I'm just the guy in charge of keeping you busy."

Stroud closed his eyes, mind drifting. "I am overwhelmed with the urge to unfurl my wings and disappear into the clouds."

"You got wings, old man?"

"How far would you chase me? How high?" Stroud asked, lost in a hallucination.

"All the way to the sun," the guard said.

"Even as the heat melted the flesh from your bones, as your eyes dissolved into liquid jelly?"

"Even then."

"Very well." The dream disintegrated, and he reopened his eyes, his wings gone forever, dissolving to vapor in the cold air behind him "Let's get on with this then."

The guard held out his hand, and Stroud accepted it, his eyes focused on his government-issued shoes and the ground that constrained them.

The Gas Chamber
by Rob Hart

The whistle went off, and Eddy fell in step with the single-file line marching into the dining hall. His stomach gnawed on itself. Between processing and a ferryboat running behind schedule, he missed breakfast.

As he passed the long row of empty cells, their occupants shuffling somewhere ahead of him, he reached out and drummed his fingers off the metal bars.

Hunger, at least, was a problem with a solution.

The dining hall made him think of his high-school cafeteria back in Utah. White paint beginning to peel, thick columns holding the ceiling up. Like it was poured and chiseled from one giant slab of concrete.

Instead of long tables with benches, the place was filled with four-top tables, many of which were already taken by inmates, sitting in plastic chairs and hunched over metal trays. The low murmur of hushed conversations and harsh metal clacking of silverware permeated the room. There were three guards strolling the gaps between the tables. That was a little different from high school, too.

Eddy watched as the inmates accepted trays of food

through a gap in the bars, from a counter that fronted the kitchen. He had expected something that only vaguely resembled food, flopped onto his plate with indifference. But when he caught sight of the menu board, he couldn't help but smile.

Split Pea Soup
Roast Pork Shoulder
Mashed Potatoes
Stewed Corn
Bread & Coffee

Eddy accepted a tray of food and a lukewarm cup of black coffee from a hatchet-faced man behind the counter. The food looked better than any meal he'd had recently. He took it and wended through the dining hall, looking for an empty seat. There weren't any in sight, and within seconds his heart was racing.

A man standing alone in a place like this probably looked a little like a target. Every second he was on his feet, he was drawing attention to himself.

He came across a table with three men and an empty seat. He paused and thought about asking if he could sit, but he didn't want that to be perceived as a sign of weakness. He pulled out the seat and sat, hoping he hadn't just made a mistake.

His skin was hot with anger and regret. This was his fault. He knew it was his fault. All he had to say was "no." Instead he said "yes."

It was a mistake he'd repay for the next ten years.

The man directly across from him, his face a topographical map of scars, slate-gray hair slicked flat to his skull, raised an eyebrow.

"Here we go," he said, his voice like a handful of gravel in a tin cup. "We needed a fourth man."

Eddy glanced at the other two men, faces down, shoveling food into their mouths. He looked at the man across from him. "For what?"

The man's eyes darted around the dining hall, focusing on the guards, who were all far enough away they couldn't hear. "For if we're going to get the hell out of here. I'm Milton, by the way."

Milton jerked a thumb at the nervous-looking man to his left with the shaved head and glasses and sweat collecting at the base of his neck. "That's Abner."

He turned the thumb and pointed it to his right to a tow-headed blond who looked like a linebacker gone to seed. "And this is Franklin."

"I'm Eddy."

Abner looked up. "Would you like to hear something interesting?"

Milton rolled his eyes, but Eddy said, "Sure."

"In Russia, prisons are called gulags," Abner said, pushing his glasses up his nose and toward his eyes. "They're not very nice. People try to escape, all the time. When they do, they bring an extra person along. Someone they can eat if they run out of food. They call that person the cow. The cow doesn't know he's the cow, but he's the cow all the same. See, if they start a fire, it would give away their location. So they eat the cow's kidneys and blood because you can eat those without cooking them."

"Jesus," Franklin said. "Kidneys and blood? You gotta say that kind of stuff while we're eating?"

Eddy suddenly didn't feel welcome. He went to stand, looking around for another free seat. "I can find a different place to sit . . ."

Milton put his hand up and motioned for Eddy to stay where he was.

"Abner thinks he's being funny," Milton said. "His kind of funny isn't most people's kind of funny. Abner, we're not in the middle of the Russian wilderness. You can see the city lights from the windows. We just have to get across the water. Believe me, that's going to be the easy part."

"It's not so easy," Abner said. "Lots of people have tried."

"We'll get to that part when we get to that part," Milton said. He turned to Eddy. "First day in?"

Eddy nodded.

"Welcome to the gas chamber," Milton said. "Eat quick. We only get twenty minutes. Move fast enough and you can get seconds. But your plate needs to be clear at the end, no matter what. You leave food on your plate, maybe they give you a warning this time, being it's your first day. Next time they start revoking privileges."

"Thanks. No one's really explained . . ."

Milton raised an eyebrow. "I said you have to eat quick."

Eddy nodded and tucked in. The soup was a touch bland, but the pork shoulder was perfectly cooked, and the mashed potatoes were among the best he ever had. He cleared half his plate before he realized the food was singeing the roof of his mouth. He was so hungry he didn't care. He paused to catch his breath and looked at the other men, who were eating with equal fervor.

"Why do you call it the gas chamber?" Eddy asked.

Franklin nodded toward a small box near the ceiling, painted white to blend into the wall. "Tear gas canister. We misbehave, guards turn 'em on."

Eddy looked around the room and saw seven he could count from his vantage point. He took a big bite of corn. Perfectly buttery and salty.

"This food is pretty boss," Eddy said. "Not what I expected."

"They got a thing about the food here," Franklin said. "They figure if it's good we won't cause trouble or try to escape."

"Little do they know . . ." Milton said, laughing.

Franklin rolled his eyes. "Okay. You obviously want to tell us. What's this plan of yours?"

Milton looked around again to make sure no one was listening. "It's well established that digging instruments are hard to come by, correct?" He glanced at Eddy. "At the end of the meal the guards check to make sure all your silverware is accounted for. Plus you have to go through a metal detector." He stuck a finger in the air. "So don't go dropping anything."

"You think a spoon is going to get you out of this place," Franklin said. "You're a kook, Milton."

"No, I am not a kook," Milton said. "I've got it all mapped out. Just need something to dig with. And I figured out how we get a spoon or two. It'll take a little time, but, you know, time is the one thing all of us have."

Everyone paused and looked at Milton, who was smiling like he would never stop.

"We bribe one of the lifers," Milton said.

Franklin huffed. "That's your plan? First you invite this stranger into the crew, like we can even trust him. Then you tell us the way to get this done is getting even more people involved?"

Milton stuck a finger in the air. "First, there are plenty of guys here with nothing to lose. Chances are whoever does it for us ends up on D-Block for a bit, but we can make it worth his while."

He put up a second finger. "Second, you got, what, eight years left?" He turned to Abner. "You got seven. That I know. I got seven, too." Milton looked at Eddy. "How many you got, kid?"

"Ten," Eddy said.

Milton winced. "Ten years in a place like this. You're in the prime of your life. You don't want to spend the prime of your life here, do you?"

"Does anyone want to be here at all?" Eddy asked.

"It's not that bad," said Abner.

"Shut up," said Milton, drawing out the words so it sounded more like "shaht ahp." "The point is . . ."

Abner made a low whistling sound like a bird. Milton fell silent, putting his head down and cramming food into his mouth. Eddy looked up and saw a colossal Easter Island statue in a guard's uniform approaching the table.

"Gentlemen," the statue said, in a way that made it sounds like he didn't think they were gentlemen.

Milton looked up and smiled. With a mouth full of food he said, "How are you today, sir."

"Missing the days when you goons weren't allowed to talk in the cafeteria," the guard said. "Used to be just the sound of silverware for twenty minutes. Music to my ears."

The guard wandered away, eyeballing another table.

Abner leaned toward Eddy. "That's Kowalski. He says that every day."

"So this theoretical and charitable lifer," Franklin said. "What's the chance he keeps his mouth shut when the guards turn the screws?" He threw a hard glance at Eddy. "What's the chance our new friend doesn't go right to a guard as soon as we're done eating? Maybe he thinks he'll get a little reward."

"I don't . . ." Eddy started.

Milton spoke over him. "Anyone here for life is going to know better than to rat." He looked directly at Eddy. "No one here is stupid enough to rat."

Eddy nodded and kept eating.

"It's like, there was this one guy," Milton said, leaning forward, dropping his voice. "Ratted out a couple of fellas who were making pruno down in the bakery. Booze supply runs out and people are clawing at the walls. It wasn't pretty. You know what they did to him?" He whistled. "It wasn't pretty, either. Face looked like the inside of a pot of chili. I get nightmares about it sometimes."

Eddy tried to swallow the food in his mouth but couldn't stop thinking about chili.

"It's too bad you don't have a pen and paper," Milton said, giving Eddy a hard stare. "This is a lot of important stuff. The kind of things you don't want to forget. You get me?"

Eddy nodded, scraping at the remnants of food on his tray. How clean was clean enough the guards wouldn't give him trouble?

He had a lot of questions. So many he didn't know where to start with them. But it was nice there were people to show him the ropes. He'd spent the last few days forgetting how to cry, so maybe this wouldn't be so bad. Hell, maybe there was a chance to get out sooner.

"I'm just saying," Milton said. "It's good to have friends in here. If you feel like you owe me anything, I'm around."

"I got it," Eddy said. "And I appreciate it."

"Do you?"

Eddy swallowed the wad of food in his mouth and nodded.

"I do," he said.

"Good," Milton said. "Looks like we're all about done here. I'll get a guard to come over so we can get the hell out of here. We can show you around a bit, Eddy. With any luck, you won't get to know this place too well."

Milton put his hand in the air and stood, Franklin and Abner standing along with him. As Abner got up, he elbowed his cup of coffee onto Eddy. The cup was mostly empty, but as the liquid splashed his gray pants, Eddy jumped a little.

"Sorry about that," Abner said, reaching down to blot at the streaks of coffee with a napkin. Eddy pushed his hand away.

"No harm," Eddy said.

The gigantic guard from earlier, Kowalski, stopped in front of the table and surveyed the four of them.

"You ladies done playing grab-ass?" he asked Abner and Eddy.

"Just an accident," Abner said.

"An accident," Eddy repeated.

Kowalski nodded and looked down at the table, mumbling to himself. When he got to Eddy's tray he stopped. "Where's your spoon, inmate?"

"It was . . . just here."

Eddy looked around the empty trays and small piles of silverware. He was sure he left it right on top—positive he did that—but there was only the fork and knife. He looked up at Milton. The way Milton was smiling made his heart climb into his throat and expand until he couldn't breathe.

"I ask again, where's the spoon, inmate."

Milton raised an eyebrow, the corner of his lip curling up and mouthed the word: "Chili."

"I . . . must not have taken one?"

"Right," the guard said, putting his catcher's mitt of a hand on Eddy's shoulder. "Let's go have a talk. See if we can't jog your memory."

As the guard led Eddy away, he heard one of his lunch companions softly calling after him:

"Mooooo . . ."

A Broken Window
by Matthew McBride

Sitting behind the wheel, he thought about shooting dope. He thought about *her*, the one true thing he had ever loved more than anything else. He thought about the way she tasted. He saw her wait for him: bathed inside the hot white glow of that syringe like a pool of rust he longed to drink; to have her live inside his thin black veins the way she did when they first met, so long ago. When the world had been small and perfect and there'd still been hope.

Worn hinges screeching as the passenger door flung open, Frank Colette, fresh from a stretch inside and determined not to go back, yelling as he fell into the seat, told Joey Knuckles to wake up and start the truck, *now,* before they both got shot.

Joey Knuckles opened his eyes when he heard his name. A name he'd both invented and self-applied. His given name had been "Joy," his Christian name, but he went by "Joey" instead. Adding the "e," insisting it had been a mistake made by the hospital on his birth certificate, though inside he cursed his mother for burdening him with that name to begin with. A name so daft and feminine in a time when men weren't born so much as made.

Why his father would have allowed this, he would never know. Not that it mattered now since he had become someone else. Not that he could ever ask either one of them. But surely they had known life would be hard for a boy with a name like that. He'd fought every day. Broke bones with his fists, broke people open, now everyone called him Joey Knuckles.

Frank slapped Joey Knuckles across the face and told him to start the engine.

"Wake up."

Joey, sitting up fast, twisting the key with his left hand while he slammed the three-speed shifter into first with his right, held the accelerator to the floor, tires barking as the truck lurched forward and died.

Frank stared at Joey, who seemed confused. Joey looked down, like he had no idea what could have happened.

"Start the truck," Frank ordered. "Start the truck, you idiot."

Joey, touching his chest, noticed his fingers wet with blood so bright it was incandescent and looked like red paint. Frank could smell it from his side of the cab.

Joey Knuckles was mumbling now, and looking to Frank as if to complain, when a bullet came through the rear window and plowed through Joey's head. It shot out of his cheek and passed through the windshield and disappeared out a small hole Frank could have stuck his pinky through if he'd have wanted to.

Stunned, turning to look behind him, Frank saw two cops fire their weapons—one crouching, the other jammed against the side of a Cadillac and using the roof for

192

support—both unloading into the back of the Ford with brutality seldom seen.

Frank, breathing fast, clutching the money to his chest, glanced at Joey Knuckles, who'd strapped his tattered brown belt around his slender arm; paper-thin skin purple and swelled, head slumped to the side as blood poured from his cheek and shards of jawbone pushed through the hole in a slick, sweet sheen like polished alabaster.

A third officer, stumbling from the same nearby diner, scorching cup of coffee sloshing in his hand, watched as the first two cops fed the air with hot smoke and burnt lead.

Crouching down as low as he could, Frank felt the bullets pound the truck. He watched the right side mirror shatter; then the rear window blew out completely and peppered his hair with glass.

Something thumped his back, and he wondered if he'd been shot.

"Okay!" he yelled. He thought he tasted blood. "I give up, for Hell's sake. *I give up!*"

When he held both hands above his head to surrender, a cop shot him through the center of his left palm and blew off two fingers and a thumb.

Screaming now, cursing, blood on his lips, he threw the door open to make a run for it, but when he swung his leg out it was blasted by a shotgun.

He tossed the bag into the street and curled up in a ball, crying out, holding his mangled hand. He pulled his right leg up to his body and closed his eyes. He thought he saw his foot lying on the ground.

It was a cool day in San Francisco as Frank Colette waited to die.

* * *

Before he'd gotten out of that truck, he looked Joey Knuckles in the eyes. He asked him if he was ready.

"Yeah, let's go."

"Sure you're okay?"

"Why you askin'?"

"Cuz you don't look okay."

"I'm fine."

With the skin of his gaunt face stretched tight across his square-framed jaws, and with his pale skin and his emaciated body, he did not look fine. But Frank trusted him. He'd always trusted him in the past, and that trust had been well placed. And though he would swear he was off the tit, Frank knew better. When he'd ask Joey if he was clean, he would say he was, but being clean was nothing Joey knew anything about, and they both knew it.

Still, Joey never used dope on the job. Not once in all the years they'd been doing stick-ups.

"You better be fine," Frank said. "*Listen:* I'm in, I'm out. Quick as I can."

"You worry 'bout you, okay? Let me worry about me."

Opening the door and climbing out, the single-barrel shotgun hidden beneath his overcoat in a wire holster of his own construction, Frank closed the door *gently,* because it liked to stick, and if something went wrong he'd be standing there getting shot at as he wrestled the handle.

Even though he was unable to open his eyes, he realized he'd been thinking instead of dreaming. With some difficulty, he lifted one eyelid to find his head wrapped in gauze. If he squinted, he could see through it: this thin, opaque filter that both freed and enslaved him.

More talk, some laughter. He was inside a room. It was very small, but he was not alone. It was hot. Standing beside his bed was a nurse with gray hair wound very tight beneath a cheap, white cap that looked too small for her head. There was a doctor beside her, talking to a plainclothes detective and a uniformed cop.

As things came into focus, Frank wondered if he was the cop who'd shot him. He wasn't. After listening to them talk, Frank learned it was the partner of the cop Frank had shot inside the bank; the cop he'd never intended to shoot in the first place, until the son of a bitch pulled his burner and Frank cut him down with the scattergun.

That was when all Hell broke loose. As he was leaving, two cops came out of nowhere—one with a white napkin, crisp and clean, unfolded, hanging from the neck of his shirt, still chewing a mouthful of something, his gun already drawn, uncocked and firing—the other attempting to unholster his weapon at a fast walk and not having much luck, until he stopped and looked down and took his time and drew.

Frank, stumbling, ears ringing, had reached again for the shotgun. But when he turned to raise it, the wire hanger broke inside his coat, and he dropped it. He'd sprinted to the truck then, leaving it to be picked up moments later by the first cop, who'd used it to shoot Frank in the leg at close range when he'd opened the door to run.

Frank coughed, and the voices inside the room became still. They knew he was awake, and in this new silence, with quick, light steps, the doctor came toward him.

Only vaguely aware of his own existence, Frank wondered if his hand was gone. And he wondered if his foot had been shot off, too, or if that had been a dream. He wondered if there was anything else missing he should know about, then he wondered how he could still be alive if there were.

"Wake up, tough guy," he heard someone say. A distant voice moving closer.

Frank flinched, not that it mattered. The top of his head was heavily bandaged. They could not see his face. They just wanted to *talk* to him. Not torture him. Talk.

The uniformed cop, who Frank could barely make out— angry, talking fast, stepping loud—passed the doctor in his hard-sole shoes then halted by Frank's bedside. He spoke about his partner and cursed his bad luck for cashing his check on lunch, not to mention Frank's own misfortune for robbing a bank next to a diner and getting shot by his own gun.

He said, "You're not very good at this."

Frank said nothing. He was so far away.

Reaching down, grabbing what was left of Frank's hand, the cop squeezed hard where his fingers once had been. Frank felt nothing. Patches of light dripped through his dressing in blonde fragments like warm dabs of honey as he floated on ten-thousand bubbles that carried his body in a dream. A dream he could sense would end soon, one he was loath to vacate. It washed over him. Transitory and short-lived and ephemeral.

"He's heavily sedated," the doctor said, annoyed. *He can't feel anything.*

"Lucky for him."

Leaning over the bed, very close now, the cop aligned his face with Frank's; his breath fetid and foul, as if some primordial creature had crawled inside his mouth long ago and shat and died and the cop never knew.

Squinting now, Frank could see him. His features old but tough; his chin was very square at the bottom. Both jaws wide. Hard and angular, as if his now distorted features had once been antediluvian stone some malevolent god used to carve him a face.

He stood up and relit a fat cigar that resembled a wet dog turd and told the doctor he should pull the plug.

"Excuse me," the doctor said, pushing his way by the cop, waving his hand in front of him to cut the smoke.

"This mook killed a cop."

"My job's to save 'em, your job's to kill 'em."

"That's right," the cop said. Thick lips bending into a broad grin.

The doctor said, "Guess you shoulda done a better job."

Both cops laughed. The detective walked out, uniformed cop behind him. The doctor, following last, turned off the lights and closed the door.

It was dark. Frank was alone. Finally. He had time to think. To find a way out. But there was no one on earth to save him, and nothing inside the room to help.

The next day there was nothing. Only his thoughts and his inner reflections and the darkness that enveloped him. Then the lights: loud fluorescent tubes that hummed and vibrated. They called to him with electric energy, like whispers from forgotten ghosts.

And then it was one of two doctors, or two, sometimes three cops: all looking to jam him up. It was the same hustle it had always been, the same one he'd been caught up in his whole life.

"Ya messed up now, pal," they said. "You're goin' back to The Rock. You know what they do to cop killers out there?"

"Give them a reward?"

Nobody laughed.

"You think you're real tough, dontcha?" said the same hard-faced cop when he came back. This time he was alone. Frank ignored him. So when he pretended to sleep, the cop lifted his nightgown and burned him with a hot cigar.

Frank shrieked. A chimney-red burn below his belly button already swelling amid small, white blisters filled with blood.

"That's what I thought," the cop said. "Hope ya got a chance to look down there 'n' see what's missin'. Guess ya won't be hitchhikin' for a while."

Eyebrows arched, shrugging at Frank's limbs suspended in air, the cop pointed. *That leg.*

Frank said he was fine, fully aware of his injuries. It was the first thing he'd taken stock of upon his awakening.

The cop said, "I guess you'll never dance again."

Frank said, "Look at the money the state will save on shoes."

The cop left the room, leaving Frank with the sounds of monitors. Later the cop returned and watched him sleep and smoked a cigar. When Frank woke, there were more cops in the room. They asked him questions he ignored. They all shook their heads: the cops in uniforms and the doctors and the detective. They told him he was dead once he went back, and Frank said he was dead already.

What he didn't tell them was that he wasn't going back, that he already had a plan. One he set in motion the day he arrived.

There was no clock in the room and no way to keep time, but at the end of what Frank could only assume was several days and after numerous surgeries—all attempts to save his foot and all of them failures—the doctor lifted Frank from his bed and set him in a worn-out chair. It was yellow and plastic and old.

Then the cop returned and said, "Ready to ride *The Warden*?"

He laughed as he smoked and asked Frank what he thought about that.

Frank said he couldn't wait. But he would not be riding *The Warden Johnston*. Not this time. He'd ridden it twice before, once on his way to The Rock and once on his way back, and he'd made a promise to himself not to take that ride again. The ferry was old, and the water was cold, and Frank hated boats to begin with since he had never learned to swim.

He sat in his chair, and he laid in his bed, and they waited 'til he was strong enough to move. When he was, the cop was the first to give him the news. News he delivered with pleasure. Delivering bad news meant a lot to a man like that in a world where nothing else meant a thing.

"We're takin' you back tomorrow," he said. "But I doubt you last 'til your court date. I hear you ain't so popular out there on account of how you left things with Stubby Thompson."

Frank swallowed. His lips cracked, and his mouth was very dry.

The cop watched him, tried to sweat him. Frank wanted water but refused to give him the satisfaction of knowing his thirst. He remained silent.

"You're gonna die out there while you wait for trial," the cop went on. "Gonna get you your old cell back—your old cellmate, too. Fact, buncha your old friends back there can't wait to see you."

That was one more reason Frank would not be going. He didn't have any old friends. Just old enemies. Alcatraz was full of them. And he *had* left things in a bad way. He'd accumulated some debts while inside, mostly gambling, and mostly to his former cellmate, Stubby, a man respected and feared, a man who once punched Al Capone in the jaw. He'd been housed there eighteen years, and that was a long time to be there and know he would not get out. He hated anyone else who did.

The cop was right. Frank Colette would not last one night on the island.

Using all of his energy, he crawled out of bed. It was dark, but after some time a thin crack of light entered the room and found him. The light was long and warm and he was sitting in the plastic chair when the doctor arrived.

That surprised him, Frank's ability to move himself like that.

"Guess you feel okay," he said.

"Never felt better."

The doctor said that was nice to hear. They had good folks out there that could use his bed. *Decent folks.*

Frank nodded. He knew he was right. Frank Colette was as indecent as they come.

Signing his name to a paper attached to a clipboard, the doctor said there was someone there to see him. *Your friend,* he said. "The partner of the cop you shot."

"You tell him I said to fuck himself."

The doctor, stunned, sucked in a mouthful of air but did not respond.

Frank looked down where his foot used to be and told him *thanks for nothin'.*

The doctor, red-faced and fuming, stomped from the room and closed the door, as Frank, standing on the only foot he had left, pulled his chair across the floor. It was fifteen steps to the window and thirty feet to the sidewalk; he'd measured them in his mind.

When he was almost there, he heard voices in the hall. A hearty round of laughter, as Frank, walking the chair out in front of him, limping, hopping, using momentum and all the strength he had, hurled the chair through the window, his stump grinding into the concrete floor, dark blood a snaking smear behind him.

Glass was still dropping from the wooden frame as the cop burst through the door. Frank leaned out the window as the cop pulled his revolver.

"You gonna shoot?"

"You gonna jump?"

Frank said he was by not saying he wasn't, and the cop put his gun away.

As he plucked splinters of glass from the framework, their eyes connected, and in one imperfect moment they saw each other for who they were.

The cop nodded.

Frank sat on the ledge and leaned back into nothing. Without looking down, without a sound, he fell.

The Music Box
by Leah Rhyne

I was eleven years old when I fell in love.

Long of limb and stuffed full of talent, I was told Mademoiselle Helene would come to Alcatraz Island to work with me, a budding ballerina, Tuesdays and Thursdays before the little girls appeared for their baby ballet class. When she stepped into the ballet studio, a makeshift deal in the big room in the Officer's Club, I stood alone at the barre, wishing for wall-to-wall mirrors so I could check the arch of my foot, the curve of my arm overhead. I was talented, they said. I could go places with my dancing. Hence Helene.

She was French, and my parents paid an exorbitant amount to convince Helene to cross the grim chop of the San Francisco Bay to work with me. They said she had danced as a soloist with a Russian company before the war. Following an escape to the States, California had been her home for a brief tenure before my parents found her and offered her employment. When they described her to me, I made a mental note to ask about her escape. It sounded dramatic. Exciting. Exactly the opposite of civilian life outside our country's most notorious penitentiary.

I gasped when Mademoiselle Helene entered the room. My foot dropped from the barre and hit the parquet floor with a dull thud.

I'd never seen Venus personified. I'd never seen a creature embody such grace. Beauty. Seduction. I'd been alive a meager eleven years, after all, and the scope of my life was limited to children playing baseball on the parade grounds. The men I encountered were old and gnarled, wearing carefully pressed uniforms. The women were ancient mothers in housedresses. Curlers.

Slender and graceful as a Victorian candelabra; therefore, Mademoiselle Helene was so different it was breathtaking. She wore an elegant wool coat and three-inch tall heels. Her hair, a brown so deep it was almost black, was cut in a French style Audrey Hepburn wouldn't make famous for a decade. High, well-defined cheekbones and almond blue eyes topped a perfect pout mouth. The milk-and-potato honed children who surrounded me on the Island were nothing beside Mademoiselle Helene.

Her smile was gentle, even shy, as she began to peel off the layers she had worn against the damp, biting chill outside. Beneath the coat were dance clothes, tight and form-hugging, pressing up against her muscular legs, Scarlet O'Hara waist, and gently curving neck. She kicked off those tall stiletto heels one at a time, and even the careless pile in which they fell was made elegant by her presence. As she wrapped the ribbon of her pointe shoes up her perfect calves, I tried to speak but found no words that would convey my instant adoration, nor my own clumsiness. Insignificance. So I stood and I stared, my heart dancing a moonlight sonata and parts of me growing damp from nervous sweat.

Mademoiselle Helene nodded at me, walked over to the record player in the corner of our small "studio," and lowered the needle. The music was from *Swan Lake*, my favorite tragic tale. Helene swayed to the strings, and then began to dance.

I lived and breathed ballet from birth. Every time a company toured in San Francisco, I begged and pleaded until my mother found a way to take me. I'd marvel at the dancers' strength. Their grace and elegance.

I'd never seen anyone dance like Mademoiselle Helene.

She didn't leap—she flew. She didn't pirouette—she cycloned. She floated on the air, weightless. She danced hard, throwing herself through the steps, and yet she remained delicate. When she was done, I realized I hadn't breathed, and tears cut down my face like a closing curtain. I exhaled a damp, rattled breath, swiping at the wetness on my face. My bare wrist did little to wash away what Mademoiselle Helene unleashed in me.

She bowed deeply and then her face burst open with a smile. "You want to dance like this, yes?" she said in an accent that oozed pheromones.

"*Oui*," I gasped, the only French word I knew.

"*Jete, jete, sissone, plié, pirouette, repetez, jete, jete* . . . *oui*, yes, *trés bon*, and *oui*, yes, good, again."

We worked for our hour, alone. Mademoiselle Helene turned my head, bent my back, and pointed my toes. She used her hands to mold me, to shape me, to turn me into something good. Something better.

I was putty in her elegant, white hands.

* * *

I stayed after our first session to watch Mademoiselle Helene with the little girls who lived on the island with their mommies and daddies, who wanted to be ballerinas just like us.

With them, she was softer. Gentler. Her accent became less severe. I loved her less as she crept through the room, patting heads and cheeks, folding tiny arms and legs into acceptable versions of first and third positions.

After class, as the echo of tiny voices faded from the room, Mademoiselle Helene pulled on her stiletto heels, coat, and scarf. I watched as she did, and when she left the Officer's Club, I followed until she beckoned for me to walk beside her.

We walked in companionable silence, student and teacher, in the long shadow of the penitentiary. We wandered down East Road, past the electric shop and toward the dock, where the ferry waited to carry her to the mainland. A tear escaped my eye, but in the wind off the water, so biting and so raw, it disappeared. I couldn't imagine a day going by without Helene, let alone the two days it would take to carry me from Tuesday to Thursday.

It was growing late, the salt in the air more insistent. Whitecaps swelled and crashed on the Bay. Her ride home would be a rocky one.

The approaching ferry bounced on the water, droplets of surf splashing and catching in our hair, as a man stood at the edge of the dock, sweeping away debris. Little boys loved playing cops and robbers on Alcatraz Island, and the paper remnants from their cap guns blew around the man's feet.

The sweeper was a prison inmate, and though I, a

longtime resident of the island, didn't often notice inmates, I noticed him. So did Mademoiselle Helene. She took my hand as we neared him, one of the storied residents of Alcatraz. She shuddered.

He was tree-like in height and arm span, an effect enhanced by his broom, its wooden handle a natural extension of his limbs. Later in life, I'd have called him an "Ent," after the towering creatures in *Lord of the Rings*, but at that time my reading was limited to *Nancy Drew* or *The Happy Hollisters*. The prisoner faced away from us, hunched over his task.

He whistled, though, and that, perhaps, was what stopped Mademoiselle Helene. It was the theme from *Swan Lake*, the song we'd danced to that afternoon. Helene began to sway beside me as the inmate's whistle trebled and trilled, a song as lovely as a mockingbird's. I, too, moved, a company member supporting my prima ballerina. My eyes met Mademoiselle Helene's, and suddenly we were conspirators in an unspoken crime. She let go of my hand, and though we wore layers over our dance clothes, we broke into our steps. *Jete, jete, sissone, plié, pirouette, repetez, jete, jete . . .*

We giggled, clumsy in our winter gear, taking joy in the simple pleasure of dancing to music whistled by a stranger.

Upon hearing our laughter, the inmate turned, and we stopped. His size wasn't the most notable thing after all. It was his mismatched, broken face. His left profile was normal, handsome even, with a sharp, clean-shaven chin and an eye of deep mahogany. But the right side? Oh, the right side. It was dizzying, blanketed with the pucker of sour pink scars and crumpled-paper flesh. His right eye was leached of all color, blind and dim, burnt crispy and never fully healed.

The whistle left his lips as Mademoiselle Helene and I froze, cold in the spotlight of his ruined gaze. His broom ceased its back and forth.

"Move on, girls, move on," said his guard, Sergeant Cooper. "Needham, get back to work."

The broom began again, and the prisoner—Needham—turned away. His whistle began again, too, though this time he switched to the "Waltz of the Snowflakes" from *The Nutcracker*. Mademoiselle Helene let go of my hand and walked down the dock. She began to dance again, becoming a wintery fairy, turning even the misting rain to snow.

Our classes continued, Tuesdays and Thursdays, throughout the winter. My dance improved beneath Mademoiselle Helene's watchful gaze and helpful hands, and my love for her grew deeper. I'd had a secret boyfriend on the island, Tommy Carlisle from down the hall in Building 64, but we'd broken off our engagement, my affections for him eclipsed by the existence of my French ballerina. Mademoiselle Helene and I had found a similar language, broken English and broken French, and though she was my teacher, we laughed together, as well, in our Officer's Club studio. I helped instruct the smaller children, and they looked up to us both, calling me "Teacher" as often as they did my Helene.

Each day after class, I walked with Mademoiselle Helene to the dock, and each day the looming Needham, was there, sweeping and whistling. We relinquished our fear of his appearance as novelty gave way to routine, and he quizzed us often, whistling different ballets for us to dance to, and even, occasionally, a popular Broadway tune. We danced to it all, our steps alternating between graceful and silly, improvising spins and leaps to work with any tune. We giggled, our hands intertwined, our skin electric. Our feelings were palpable, and although we never spoke of it, I was sure Helene loved me as I did her. Could she hold me the way she did when we danced for Needham, if she didn't? Would she look as she did, her eyes wide and liquid, when he whistled a sad tune, if she wasn't aware we were about to part?

We never spoke to Needham. Interaction with inmates was forbidden under the gaze of Sergeant Cooper. We pushed the limits of his patience simply by dancing, but dance we did. To us, Needham was our music box, and we were his spinning ballerinas.

It was February, cold and damp, when I developed pneumonia. Barred from school, banned from dance class, I was locked away like a fairy-tale princess without another princess to rescue me. I missed two weeks of dancing with Mademoiselle Helene, and by the third Tuesday, I was antsy. Grouchy. Still not allowed to dance.

I missed my love. The way she moved. The way she held me when I fell. The way she clapped her hands when I particularly pleased her.

So when the phone rang in the front room of my apartment, fifteen minutes before the ferry on which Mademoiselle Helene would depart, and when my mother's face lit up upon hearing *her* mother's voice (long distance!), I knew I had a shot. While she was occupied, I pulled on a coat and snuck out the front door.

The cold was a punch in my broken lungs when I stepped outside Building 64, avoiding the stares of busybody mothers pushing babies in hand-me-down prams. I held in my cough and set off on the walkway to the dock.

The sky was frozen steel, our own prison bars. A light mist fell, salted and sharp. I shuddered. The sun sank low behind the prison walls; it was getting on toward shift change, toward dinner, toward night. I hurried, anxious to see Mademoiselle Helene, to confess my love, to apologize for my long absence. She needed me. She missed me like I missed her.

As I hurried along, I imagined our moment. She'd be standing on the dock where we danced, watching the ferry as it rose and fell on the rumbling waves. Her hand would rest on the rail as she shivered, alone. Her face would brighten when she saw me. She'd run to me on impossibly long legs, and I'd fall into her arms. "*Ma Cherie*," she'd say, holding me, our hearts pressed together and beating as one.

I smiled despite the burning of each breath in my ailing chest.

I approached the dock, where my first sight was Needham. He stood apart from the hustle of workers hurrying aboard to get home for dinner, swishing his broom slowly back and forth. His lips, though, were still. Silent. Pressed together in a thin line I was unfamiliar with.

I skidded to a halt as a mournful sound rode in on the wind. Someone was singing. There were no words, though, just notes drifting through the air like snowflakes.

I turned to find the source of the song. Deep in the shadow of the prison walls, but still within sight of the dock, and within the gaze of Needham, with his broom and his scars, was Mademoiselle Helene. Singing. Dancing. In only her thin dance clothes and pointe shoes, her coat and heels discarded beside a shrub. She sang and performed a variation of the *pas de deux* in *Giselle,* in which Giselle, dead, dances for her lost love, to tell him her feelings will thrive beyond the grave.

Mademoiselle Helene danced slower than I'd seen her. More seductively. Each move dripped desire and an intimacy with an invisible partner, a love either lost or found.

I saw then that Needham was devouring her with his good eye, as his tongue caressed his charred, flaking lips. Sergeant Cooper looked elsewhere, seemingly to give them privacy. Yes. Mademoiselle Helene danced for Needham. Not for the guard. Not for me.

I knew Needham loved her. It poured out of him like waves, like the ferry returning him home. He, a criminal, an inmate at the Alcatraz Penitentiary, now filled the air with a love so stifling I could not breathe.

Helene reached the climax of her dance, her singing growing louder and stronger along with her *grande jetes.* Now people on the dock stopped to stare. Their bustle slowed, and the hum ceased, until there was no one moving but Mademoiselle Helene.

She ended her solo with a pirouette, an arabesque, and finally, a bow.

The dock erupted in applause, and Mademoiselle Helene looked abashed. She hadn't noticed them; she had only danced for him.

And then she found me, standing at the edge of the crowd. She reached out. "Flora," she called, as though to stop me. "Flora, *s'il vous plait . . .*"

I turned. I ran. My broken heart would never dance again.

Leah Rhyne

* * *

Spring in San Francisco was very blue and green that year. I was walking down Folsom Street one day after school when I saw Mademoiselle Helene for the first time since her so loon the dock. She tripped gaily down the other side of Folsom, as breathtakingly beautiful as ever. Doubly-so, backlit by a ray of springtime sun.

No, I won't talk to her, I thought. Better to stay away, to not let her know that she'd broken my heart into a thousand puzzle pieces that could never be reassembled. But still I crossed the street, the better to see her, ducking behind a car to make sure I remained unnoticed.

Sometimes life is kind. Sometimes a chance encounter with the love of one's life ends only in a forgotten, fleeting glance, a mild hummingbird's thrum of one's heart. But other times life is cruel.

I neared Helene, drawing up behind her. For a moment, my hand ached as I marched in rhythm with her graceful steps, my thick school skirt nothing to her swinging spring dress. I almost reached out to hold her hand like so many times before. But I didn't. Perhaps I should have, but from the dark shadow between two buildings, another hand emerged, scarred, the skin puckered and diseased.

I knew that hand.

I'd watched it wield a broom often during my weeks with Mademoiselle Helene. It grabbed her, pulling her into the shadow. Mademoiselle Helene cried out, a sound that was stifled so quickly I was certain no one heard but me.

I followed her into the darkness. Needham, the whistling inmate, now relinquished of his broom and free, stood against the wall, his hand on her heart, hers on his.

212

"Mine," he growled, in a voice as broken and gravely as his face. A voice so incongruous with the fleeting beauty of his whistling, I blinked and rubbed my eyes to be sure of what I was seeing. I have never been entirely sure.

"You're finally mine."

Mademoiselle Helene's eyes widened. I watched in silence as Needham pulled her further into the shadows.

I was a girl without a teacher. I was nothing.

"S'il vous plaît," she said.

I would never dance again.

Live at Alcatraz
by Nick Kolakowski

The Man in Black lights his tenth cigarette of the morning, his blood crackling electric, and wishes he had swallowed another couple pills with his coffee. Maybe it's how the boat rocks in the hard chop of the Bay, or maybe it's the way one of the guards onboard keeps looking at him like a cockroach, but his stomach feels ready to hit the eject button. Cigarette pasted in the corner of his mouth, a draw of smoke tingling his lungs, he clenches his hands into fists.

"You okay, chief?" asks Luther Perkins, his guitarist, from the neighboring bench. When he's onstage, Perkins is the anchor that keeps the Man in Black from spinning out of control. But on this bucking ferry, he seems a little panicked, almost tumbling from his seat.

"Nothing good about a prison you can't walk out of." The Man in Black nods across the water, toward the dark silhouette of the island off starboard. From a half-mile out, they can already see the tiny windows stitching the concrete cellhouse atop that slab of rock. Behind those windows, he knows, men in chains watch their approach. Waiting. Wanting. Aching for any scrap of hope.

Perkins offers a tight smile. "Nothing good about a prison at all."

The Man in Black destroys his cigarette in four long pulls and tosses it over the side. His tongue tastes like burnt iron. The three diet pills with breakfast are usually enough stimulant to crush any crows of doubt flying around his skull, fill him with the lightning to stride onstage and blast the walls down with the power of his baritone. Not this morning, though. The dark birds still roost in the bone prison behind his eyes, pecking at his thoughts, making his guts lurch.

"Chief?" Perkins leans forward, brow furrowed with concern. The Man in Black waves him off and shifts his view to the foredeck, where the guard with the bright red face keeps trying to stare him down. The meanness in the man's eyes reminds him of those hard sharecroppers back in Arkansas, the ones who lived and died alongside his Daddy. In another life, he might have become someone like that, holding a shotgun on his fellow sinners. Instead, the angels filled his fingers with grace, and the Lord offered him the chance to lift souls up.

"We gotta do this," the Man in Black says, and stands on trembling knees, sweat stinging his eyes. Something flaps across his vision, fast and black, and he grips the railing. "We gotta."

Perkins also stands, placing a warm hand on his shoulder. "Be strong."

"With God's help." The Man in Black straightens, feeling a little livelier.

Ten minutes later, the ferry bumps against the concrete dock. Three guards await them, caps and guns glinting in the summer sun. The Man in Black waves, and none wave back. He resists the temptation to flash his middle finger. No sense in starting things off on the wrong foot. He lights a fresh cigarette as the band begins to wrestle their gear off the boat.

Moving in well-rehearsed sync, the guards step forward to unzip bags, shake instruments, open the panels on the recording equipment. They pat down every member of the band and the recording crew, the Man in Black grinning as they jam their hands in his pockets, feel his cuffs, make him strip off his shoes. *Left all my good stuff at home, boys,* he thinks. *This ain't my first rodeo.*

When the guards finish their search, a bird-faced fellow in a decent suit appears at the far end of the dock. His hard stance and pursed lips remind the Man in Black of tax collectors, government agents, recording-label executives. A type he doesn't like, in other words.

"I'm Warden Blackburn," the man announces. "I'm going to be direct with you: I believe the inmates on this island are entitled to food, water, a roof, and medical attention when necessary. *Not* entertainment. But I've been persuaded, let us say, to let you perform."

"That's mighty big of you," the Man in Black says. He remembers a similar speech from the screws at Folsom and San Quentin.

"The administrators tell me it might lessen some of the pressure on the cellblock," Blackburn continues. "The men have been tense lately. But I know your history, mister, and I'm here to tell you: if you do anything to encourage their antisocial tendencies, or your own, I will end the concert immediately, do you understand?"

"Yessir, bossman," the Man in Black says, suddenly convinced this prick can sniff the chemicals sweating out of his pores.

"*Live at Alcatraz*," the warden snorts. "What kind of name is that for a record?"

"My last one," the Man in Black says as he stoops, grabs the handle of his long guitar case, and strides toward the looming hulk of the prison.

The band is halfway through the third song when everything goes to hell.

Two hundred inmates line the long benches and tables of the Mess Hall, hollering and hooting as the Man in Black tears ass through the music, playing the finale of his fastest song, a blistering tune about the Rock Island Railroad Line, even more breakneck than usual, like a truck barreling down a rutted dirt road, the band behind him scrambling to keep pace. Hunched over his guitar, fingers blurring as he rides the notes, he fails to see the tattooed man leap atop the dining table to his left.

Only when the inmate roars with high-octane rage does the Man in Black glance up, taking in the coal-dark eyes, the bald skull etched with scars, the words and flames inked on the muscular forearms. In one gnarled hand, the tattooed man holds a sharpened toothbrush handle, which he jams hard into the neck of a seated inmate.

The stabbed prisoner tumbles backward with a gurgling squawk that the whole room hears over the clash of the band losing its rhythm, their train jumping the rails.

Within seconds, the Mess Hall explodes into a storm of furious bodies. Screams of fear buried under howls of triumph. The Man in Black sees two guards near the barred portal to the kitchen dragged down by a grasping sea of hands. Through the blur of running legs, he spies bodies on the scuffed linoleum, leaking red.

"Let's go. These boys ain't fans of what we're playing," the Man in Black announces, oddly calm, as he juts his chin for the band to skedaddle.

He doesn't need to tell them twice. Because they are seasoned road musicians to the bitter end, they hold tight to their instruments as they sprint for the nearest doorway. A lanky inmate with a shock of red hair charges at the Man in Black, who rears back and lashes out with his left leg, planting a boot in the redhead's stomach that sends him flailing to the floor. Marshall Grant swings his bass like an axe, shattering it along with another inmate's nose. One of the recording boys brandishes a microphone stand, clearing a path through the wide corridor outside the Mess Hall, which the guards call Times Square on account of the large clock looming on the wall.

Only when they clear the room does the Man in Black realize his hands are still strumming the guitar strings on autopilot, the chords echoing off damp concrete and steel. A long sprint down the cellblock ends at the doors that lead to the armory, a squad of panicked guards and administrators joining the flight to freedom, a wave of inmates on their heels.

The guards in the towers lay down some covering fire as the band bursts into the sunlight and sea air. Grant falls to his knees in the dirt and praises Jesus. The Man in Black looks around and realizes Perkins is nowhere to be seen. He hears the doors behind them slam shut.

* * *

"I'm going back in," the Man in Black tells the warden.

Blackburn shakes his head. "There's no chance. They'll take you hostage. And they already captured four of my guards in there."

"He's my friend," the Man in Black says. He needs all the friends he can get these days.

"I hear you. I do. But you're going to leave this to the professionals." The warden raises his arms, framing the scene. A small army of guards and San Francisco cops are swarming the parade ground below the cellhouse. More officers stream in from the dock, a few doing double-takes when they recognize the Man in Black, then pausing to ask for autographs before disappearing down the path that leads to the powerhouse on the other side of the island.

The inmates have cracked the gun lockers, and every few minutes a wild-eyed face appears in one of the small windows above, followed by the *pop!* of a pistol or the *boom!* of a rifle. Whenever this happens, the law returns a hurricane of fire, the prison walls bursting with rock and dust. As the warden murmurs about professionalism and duty, the Man in Black angles his ears to the pair of officers standing a few yards to his right.

"We'll cut a hole in the roof and toss a grenade or two down," one of the cops says. "Just like we did the bunkers in Korea."

His friend seems intrigued by the idea. "Think they'll let us do it?"

The first cop snorts. "Someone's gotta do something. Come on."

The Man in Black knows if this plan happens, the

chances of Perkins surviving drop to zero. He turns and scans the rows of nervous cops loaded with rifles, pistols, and clubs. He glances down at himself, pale and trembling, his beautiful black suit speckled with dust and blood.

Grant walks over, the recording boys trailing behind him, their dreams of the ultimate live album erased and taped over with thoughts of self-preservation. "What we gonna do, boss?"

As if on cue, the Man in Black bends over and vomits a hot load onto the gravel between his feet. Wipes his mouth clean and stands again, head throbbing like a rotten tooth. Not from pill withdrawal, although that beast is surely coming if he doesn't score soon. No, it's guilt over splitting up the band.

"You're all to stay down here and do nothing," the warden tells Grant. "Do you understand?"

Finally responding with his middle finger, the Man in Black turns on his heel and marches back down the road that leads to the cellhouse. Cops holler at him to halt and take cover, but nobody moves to stop him. Maybe they know a divine mission when they see one.

Lord, he thinks, *if you're listening, you better protect me in there. Otherwise you're gonna have my ugly ass belting out hymns for you real soon.*

Gray smoke fills the narrow corridor like ghosts, rendering the world muffled and indistinct. The Man in Black hears shouting in the distance, sometimes broken by high-pitched squeals and flashes of orange flame. It's like staring into the depths of a volcano.

The tunnel feeds into the concrete immensity of the cellblock, and here the air is a little clearer. The cell doors stand open, the tiers empty. Bits of flaming paper dance on the ocean breeze from the shattered windows.

"Hey."

The Man in Black cranes his head and spots a lone inmate on the second tier, leaning on a railing: a kid, relaxed, his eyes far older than his face. Too many young ones in places like this. It makes the Man in Black's heart break just thinking about it. He'd write a song right there if he had more time.

"I know you," the inmate says, and grins.

The Man in Black returns the grin he knows so well. "And I know you."

"You should be outside." The kid's lips tighten, his face a hard mask again. "It's safe out there."

"My guitarist's in here somewhere," the Man in Black says. "Never leave a friend behind, son. First rule of life. Especially if the show ain't over."

The kid nods and reaches into his waistband, pulling out a ragged strip of metal with a crude wooden handle. "You want this? It'll reach the heart."

The Man in Black shakes his head. "Not my style. That big fella with the tattoos, the one who started this whole ruckus, who was he?"

"That's Oates. In for murder. They put him in solitary for a couple years, then he comes out crazy as a shithouse rat, preaching about the devil. Guess you saw a bit of that."

Gunfire slaps the outside of the building. Glass shatters somewhere above their heads. Time is running out. "Where is everyone?" asks the Man in Black.

The kid shrugs. "Nobody's moved from the Mess Hall. Easier to defend. Me? I'm just looking for anything good." His left hand disappears behind his back, before reappearing like a magic trick, full of white and crimson pills.

Sweat bursts from the Man in Black's forehead. A monkey twists his stomach into a knot, reminding him of some very basic needs, and his most important meal of the day.

"Toss a couple of those vitamins down here, son."

Sweet Lord, the bennies or black beauties or bug juice or whatever else that con had been peddling make him feel ten feet tall, add four hundred pounds of muscle to his chest and arms. He imagines his guitar exploding in his hands if he tried to play it. The ravens are no longer trapped inside his head: now they flutter around his shoulders, hovering in his vision, content to witness rather than provoke. At the entrance to the Mess Hall, the lanky inmate with the red hair leaps forward for round two, unleashing a short jab that only whiffs air before the Man in Black's right boot sends him flying into the wall with the greatest of ease.

The Man in Black stops in the doorway, looks down at his feet. A bright orange glow seeps from the gaps between the tiles. When he sniffs the air, he smells sulfur. Hell is right beneath them, he realizes, pushing through like magma. He takes a deep breath and lets its heat fill him like a balloon, inflating him another two feet taller, his shadow even taller than that, looming monstrous on the concrete, as he prepares to face his last audience.

In the center of the room, the inmates have pushed together the tables. Atop that wide platform sits a chair, and in the chair sits Oates, naked, his eyes practically pinwheeling, his skin coated with dry, dark blood. His crusted right hand holds four leather leashes, which collar the necks of four naked guards kneeling before him.

"Having a little party, huh?" the Man in Black says, catching the panicked gaze of one of the guards. The tough guy from the ferry, in fact, trembling now, his cheeks glistening with tears. The Man in Black gives him a wink.

Behind Oates stand two hundred inmates in various states of undress. They hold knives and rifles and pipes ripped from the walls. In the flickering red glow from the floor, they look like spooked cattle anticipating their slaughter. The Man in Black feels an incredible sadness for the men, like a lead weight pushing through his guts. A need to sing their stories. He buries it for now. His band is his concern.

"I'm here for my man," he says.

Oates bares yellow teeth, and sweat stings the Man in Black's eyes. In the haze of the riot and the glut of pills, he's convinced he sees Oates' forehead bulging until it splits. Horns pushing out, black and gleaming.

The Man in Black licked a frog once when he was a boy, then stared at the sun to burn away the hallucinations. He's convinced that those horns drip the same poison.

"We'll trade," he says. "A life for a life. Want him to walk out? You stay behind."

"Why don't we all walk out?" The Man in Black feels his legs start to quake. The pills can conjure up a fearsome adversary, but they can pump only so much courage into his bloodstream. "Nobody wants to die today."

"See, that's where you're wrong," Oates growls, and one of the guards at his feet whines with fear. "Those of us who die today are on the first boat to Valhalla, the paradise for warriors. Do you believe that? You'd better. I saw it in a vision. In the hole."

"No shit?" The Man in Black finally spots Perkins in the crowd, his hands pinned behind his back by an inmate but otherwise looking okay. The sight of his guitarist trying to smile through the apocalyptic mayhem sends a pile-driver into the Man in Black's doubt, shattering it for good. *We can do this,* he thinks. *We can finish this show.*

Standing tall in the spot where, an eternity ago, he kicked off what he thought would be the first of his farewell tours, the Man in Black fills his chest with the burning wind.

When the strength hums in his veins, he tells the men kneeling before him, "I know a lot of you get told by everyone that you're in here because you did a bad thing. That you crossed a line. I'm not here to moralize at you. I can only tell you there's a better path because I've been in your shoes. I'm the biggest sinner in this building, bigger than this goddamned pretender."

It works. His voice moves the universe, or at least the ceiling, which bursts open with a crack that makes the inmates cry out like churchgoers in the grip of grace. Bright sunlight spears down. The Man in Black hovers between the hellfire of the riots below and the heavenly glow above, and he raises that deep voice made magic by a thousand hard nights in concert halls and prisons, and he preaches to those men:

"As a sinner and a pill-popper and a boozer and a fighter, I know how good it feels to be bad, but that's the wrong road. It gets you nothing. It leads to nothing. But there's a better path. It starts right here in this Mess and goes out those doors. It leads right to the light. So come with me now. Let's try and be better human beings in the eyes of the Lord."

At this, Oates rises from his throne, eyes wide, horns flashing red and black like a railroad crossing as he jabs a finger at the Man in Black and bellows so loud it would have done an Arkansas preacher proud. Stepping forward, he trumpets about cleansing blood and Valhalla again. Threads of drool dangle from his lips as he offers to cut the Man in Black's liver out and wring the whiskey from it as a favor.

Only none of the inmates are listening. Every eye in the room has locked on heaven above, from which an offering descends: an egg, that symbol of rebirth, shining, holy.

Not exactly an egg.

A grenade.

Perkins breaks free and runs for it, the Man in Black pushing him along as they both sprint down the corridor that connects Times Square with the blessed outside. Birds swirling through the smoke, an infernal cocktail of chemicals and adrenaline powering the Man in Black's feet like car pistons. They reach the armory just as Oates roars, followed by a muffled explosion that shakes the building and their feet.

They stumble into sunlight, cops rushing forward to help, and a moment later out come the naked guards with the mad-dog collars still around their necks, followed by dazed and bloodied prisoners in a panicked parade. Cut and bruised and broken but not a serious injury among them. It's a certified miracle.

Or maybe not. Before the guards drag him away, the kid from the cellblock grips the Man in Black's elbow and yells, "Oates threw himself on the grenade!"

Six ounces of explosive sent the devil straight home, he thinks. *His Earthly meat absorbing most of the shrapnel in the process, thank God.*

The Man in Black notes the white wings over the kid's shoulder before he disappears into the crowd, or maybe it was the egret flapping to balance itself on the rocks in the distance.

Egret, he thinks, already writing another song. *Rhymes with regret . . .*

"I like a man who'll die for his beliefs," the Man in Black tells his guitarist, who chuckles and pulls a pack of cigarettes from his gritty coat pocket. They have a few minutes to stand and smoke, admiring the scale of the chaos, before the warden strides over, face screwed in confusion.

"I ought to have you arrested," the warden says, a neck vein throbbing like a ticking bomb. "But I suspect my bosses will want to throw a rug over this whole incident. If you keep quiet about what happened here, I believe they would be content to let you walk away."

The Man in Black sighs, knowing his final prison concert album will never see the light of day. Maybe everyone seeing the light will just have to do.

"Bossman, you shoulda stuck with 'thank you,'" the Man in Black says. "But just this once, I'll do you a favor and keep my fat mouth shut."

The warden shields his eyes from the dust and kicks at some rubble, still grappling with the situation. "This is the worst day of my life."

The Man in Black shrugs and looks out over the water toward that red bridge on the horizon, that shining Golden Gate, and the lights of civilization beyond.

"Can't help you with that. But we gave them all one hell of a show."

ABOUT THE AUTHORS

Glenn Gray's stories have appeared in a wide range of print and online publications and anthologies. Beyond his writing career, Glenn is a practicing physician specializing in Radiology. He lives in New York. His debut story collection, *The Little Boy Inside and Other Stories,* (Concord Epress) was released in 2013.

Amber Sparks is the author of *The Unfinished World and Other Short Stories,* as well as the collection *May We Shed These Human Bodies,* and co-author of *The Desert Places* with Robert Kloss and Matt Kish. Her fiction and non-fiction has appeared in numerous magazines and journals. She lives in Washington, DC with two beasts and two humans, and she lives online at www.ambernoellesparks.com or @ambernoelle. She's almost certainly seen more Godzilla movies than you.

Nick Mamatas is the author of several novels, including the San Francisco zombie apocalypse *The Last Weekend,* and the murder mystery *I Am Providence.* His short fiction has appeared in *Best American Mystery Stories, West Coast Crime Wave,* and many other anthologies and magazines.

Les Edgerton is an ex-con, matriculating at Pendleton Reformatory for burglary (plea-bargained down from multiple counts of burglary, armed robbery, strong-armed robbery and possession with intent). He was an outlaw for many years, involved in shootouts, knifings, robberies, high-speed car chases, drug-dealing, was a pimp, worked for an escort service, starred in porn movies, was a gambler, and other misadventures. Work of his has been nominated for or won: the Pushcart Prize, O. Henry Award, Edgar Allan Poe Award (short story category), Derringer Award, PEN/Faulkner Award, Jesse Jones Book Award, Spinetingler Magazine Award for Best Novel, and the Violet Crown Book Award, among others He holds the MFA in Writing from Vermont College.

Rory Costello is, as one might expect, a Civil War buff. His crime fiction has been published in *Out of the Gutter Online.* He also contributed to *Waiting to Be Forgotten,* the anthology of stories inspired by the songs of The Replacements.

Jedidiah Ayres has some books and a blog.

Michael Paul Gonzalez is the author of the novels *Angel Falls* and *Miss Massacre's Guide to Murder and Vengeance.* A member of the Horror Writers Association, his short stories have appeared in print and online, including *Lost Signals, HeavyMetal. com, Drive-In Creature Feature, Gothic Fantasy: Chilling Horror Stories, 18 Wheels of Horror,* and the *Booked. Podcast Anthology.* He resides in Los Angeles, a place full of wonders and monsters far stranger than any that live in the imagination. You can visit him online at MichaelPaulGonzalez.com.

Carrie Laben grew up in western New York and earned her MFA at the University of Montana. She now lives in Queens. She blogs at *10,000 Birds,* and her work has appeared or is forthcoming in such venues as *Montana Naturalist, The Dark, Indiana Review, Okey-Panky,* and the anthology *Mixed Up!* In 2015 she was selected for the Anne LaBastille Memorial Writer's Residency.

Johnny Shaw is the author of the "Jimmy Veeder Fiasco" series which includes the novels, *Dove Season, Plaster City,* and *Imperial Valley,* as well as the stand-alone novels *Big Maria* and *Floodgate.* His short stories have appeared in *Thuglit, Plots With Guns, Shotgun Honey, Crime Factory, Blood & Tacos,* and numerous anthologies. Johnny has won the Anthony Award and two Spotted Owl Awards. He lives in Portland, Oregon.

Mark Rapacz's stories have appeared in a number of publications, including *Plots with Guns, Revolver, Thuglit, Dark Corners, The Booked. Anthology, Water-Stone Review, East Bay Review, Martian Lit, The Best American Nonrequired Reading,* and many others. His latest novel, *Boondoggle,* is out now from 280 Steps. He and his wife live in Minneapolis where he continues to write stories.

Joshua Chaplinsky is the Managing Editor of LitReactor.com. He has also written for the popular film site Screen Anarchy and for ChuckPalahniuk.net, the official website of *Fight Club* author Chuck Palahniuk. He is the author of *Kanye West—Reanimator.* His short fiction has appeared in *Zetetic, Motherboard, Vol. 1 Brooklyn, Thuglit, Dark Moon Digest, Cracked Eye, Pantheon Magazine, Fabula Argentea,* and multiple print anthologies. More info at joshuachaplinsky.com.

Nik Korpon is the author of *The Rebellion's Last Traitor* (Angry Robot, 2017) and *The Soul Standard,* among others. He lives in Baltimore.

Gabino Iglesias is a writer, journalist, and book reviewer living in Austin, TX. He's the author of *Zero Saints* (Broken River Books), *Hungry Darkness* (Severed Press), and *Gutmouth* (Eraserhead Press). His reviews have appeared in *Electric Literature, The Rumpus, 3AM Magazine, Marginalia, The Collagist, Heavy Feather Review, Crimespree, Out of the Gutter, Vol. 1 Brooklyn, HorrorTalk, Verbicide,* and many other print and online venues. You can find him on Twitter at @Gabino_Iglesias.

When not scribbling twisted musings into spiral notebooks, photographing the odd puddle or junk pile, or building classy furniture, Dino Parenti earns a little scratch drawing buildings. His work can be found in a several anthologies, as well as the following journals: *Menacing Hedge, Pantheon Magazine, Cease-Cows, Pithead Chapel,* and *Lascaux Review,* where he won their first annual flash fiction contest.

Max Booth III was raised in Northern Indiana and now lives in the forgotten basement of a hotel somewhere in the surreal void of Texas. He's the Editor-in-Chief of Perpetual Motion Machine and the Managing Editor of *Dark Moon Digest.* Although he's never been to prison, his face has been slammed into a cop car's hood exactly twice, so he's basically the same as anyone who's done time in Alcatraz. His latest novel is *The Nightly Disease.* Follow him on Twitter @GiveMeYourTeeth or visit him at www.TalesFromTheBooth.com.

Rob Hart is the author of *New Yorked,* nominated for an Anthony Award for Best First Novel, as well as *City of Rose* and *South Village.* He is also the publisher at MysteriousPress.com and the class director at LitReactor. His short stories have appeared in publications like *Thuglit, Needle, Shotgun Honey, Joyland,* and *Helix Literary Magazine.* Non-fiction has appeared in *The Daily Beast, Salon, The Literary Hub, Nailed,* and *Electric Literature.* You can find him online at www.robwhart.com.

Matthew McBride is a former assembly-line worker currently living in an undisclosed location. He is the author of the novels *Frank Sinatra in a Blender* and *A Swollen Red Sun.*

Leah Rhyne is a Jersey girl who's eking out a life in the South. She writes horror and science fiction. Her novel *Heartless* was released in May 2016 via Polis Books, and her short fiction has appeared in such publications as *Abyss & Apex Magazine* and *Dirge Magazine.* She lives in Charleston with her husband and daughter.

Nick Kolakowski lives and writes in New York City. His crime fiction has appeared in *Thuglit, Shotgun Honey, Out of the Gutter,* and other venues; he is also the author of the novella *A Brutal Bunch of Heartbroken Saps.* His favorite Johnny Cash song is "God's Gonna Cut You Down," which describes his mindset most days.

David James Keaton's award-winning work has appeared in over 50 publications. He is the author of *Fish Bites Cop! Stories to Bash Authorities* (Comet Press), which was named the 2013 Short Story Collection of the Year by *This Is Horror.* He is also the author of *Pig Iron* (Burnt Bridge), *Stealing Propeller Hats from the Dead* (Perpetual Motion Machine Publishing), and *The Last Projector* (Broken River Books). He lives and teaches in Santa Clara, California.

Joe Clifford is acquisitions editor for Gutter Books and producer of Lip Service West, a "gritty, real, raw" reading series in Oakland, CA. He is the author of several books, including *Junkie Love* and the Jay Porter series. Joe's writing can be found at www.joeclifford.com.

Escape From Alcatraz Island

Race through the maze and outrun the ghosts of Alcatraz Island!

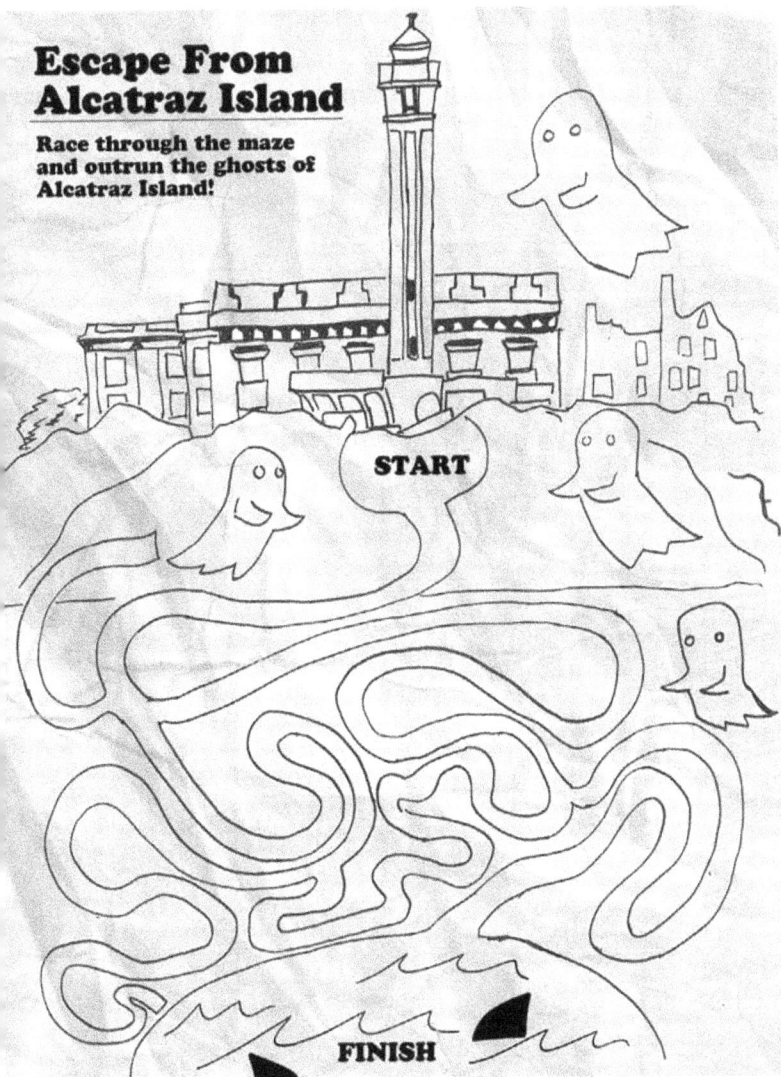

START

FINISH

"It's mighty good to get up and leave. This Rock ain't no good for nobody."

— Frank Weatherman
second-to-last inmate to leave Alcatraz Island,
March 21, 1963

www.ingramcontent.com/pod-product-compliance
Lightning Source LLC
Chambersburg PA
CBHW021616270326
41931CB00008B/732